HORIZON

MAY, 1963 · VOLUME V, NUMBER 5

HORIZON

A Magazine of the Arts

MAY, 1963 · VOLUME V, NUMBER 5

PUBLISHER
James Parton

EDITORIAL DIRECTOR
Joseph J. Thorndike, Jr.

EDITOR
William Harlan Hale
MANAGING EDITOR
Eric Larrabee
ASSOCIATE EDITOR
Ralph Backlund
ASSISTANT EDITORS
Jane Wilson
Albert Bermel, Shirley Abbott
CONTRIBUTING EDITOR
Margery Darrell
EDITORIAL ASSISTANTS
Caroline Backlund
Wendy Buehr, Priscilla Flood
COPY EDITOR
Mary Ann Pfeiffer
Assistants: Joan Rehe, Ruth H. Wolfe

ART DIRECTOR
Irwin Glusker
Associate Art Director: Elton Robinson

ADVISORY BOARD
Gilbert Highet, *Chairman*
Frederick Burkhardt   Oliver Jensen
Marshall B. Davidson   Jotham Johnson
Richard M. Ketchum   John Walker

EUROPEAN CONSULTING EDITOR
J. H. Plumb
Christ's College, Cambridge

EUROPEAN BUREAU
Gertrudis Feliu, *Chief*
11 rue du Bouloi, Paris

HORIZON is published every two months by American Heritage Publishing Co., Inc. Executive and editorial offices: 551 Fifth Ave., New York 17, N.Y. HORIZON welcomes contributions but can assume no responsibility for unsolicited material.

All correspondence about subscriptions should be addressed to: HORIZON Subscription Office, 379 West Center St., Marion, Ohio.

Single Copies: $4.50
Annual Subscriptions: $21.00 in the U.S. & Can.
$22.00 elsewhere

An annual index is published every September, priced at $1. HORIZON is also indexed in the *Readers Guide to Periodical Literature.*

Title registered U.S. Patent Office

Second-class postage paid at New York, N.Y., and at additional mailing offices.

COVER: During the 1870's Winslow Homer created many an indelible image of bustled, hatted, and neatly shod young women strolling by the sea, but in this detail from *On the Beach* the ladies have at last removed their shoes. Homer was one of the first artists to discover the charms of eastern Long Island, but *he* went out there to paint the ocean; those who live there now—as the article beginning on page 4 attests—paint anything but. Thus do art and fashion change; today a bustle on the beach would draw more stares than a bikini. The painting, one of Homer's most charming in the genre, dates from about 1870 and is in the Canajoharie (N. Y.) Library and Art Gallery.

FRONTISPIECE: An elephant's chief assets in battle were his terrifying appearance and thick hide, and this nightmarish suit of armor (worn by a pachyderm draftee at the Battle of Plassey in 1757) was designed to reinforce both. Made of steel plates linked with chain mail, and padded underneath, it could stop the relatively soft bullets of the period—but made a slippery seat for the mahout and the warrior or two perched on top. After his victory at Plassey, Lord Clive brought it back to England, where it may now be seen on an imitation elephant in "The New Armouries" of the Tower of London.

Where the avant-garde, the old guard, and the Coast Guard meet, there is held

Far Out on

a summer's spree of art and invigoration

Long Island

What brings the faithful back to the eastern end of Long Island summer after summer? The sea, the sun, the peerless beaches,
the uncrowded space, the reminders of an
earlier America (the windmill at the right
is one of several still standing in the area,
though not always on their original sites).
Also, it's cool out there—and the fact that
it is only two to three hours distant from
the tropical discomfort of summertime New
York makes it a good place for creative
people to work as well as relax. Thus the
theatrical producer Alfred de Liagre, Jr.,
can bask in the sun at East Hampton even
while he is studying the script of a play he
hopes to do next fall. Last season he was
coproducer of Peter Ustinov's Photo Finish.

By WILLIAM K. ZINSSER

Unlike the yellow brick road that meanders through Oz, the Montauk Highway does not lead to an amiable wizard. It is not even a proper highway; it is full of jagged turns where a driver least expects them. But to those who follow it out the remote southern fork of Long Island it has definite magic powers.

The motorist from Manhattan, after driving almost two hours across Long Island's dreary interior, is more than ready for magic, and when he reaches the Highway his spirit quickens. Salt air reactivates a nose deadened by urban fumes. Small roadside stands with crudely lettered signs— BAIT, FLOUNDER, STEAMERS, LOCAL VEG—remind him that food comes from the sea and the soil, not the supermarket.

The homes have no hint of Suburbia or of the glossy Exurbs. This is the look of rural America: the people are small-town merchants or truck farmers or fishermen, and many of their houses are several hundred years old, plain shingled buildings that survive from the early English settlers. As final proof that the city is now far behind, duck farms sprawl along the successive inlets, each an infinity of white feathers. Obviously "roast Long Island duckling," that hardy staple of the American hotel menu, is in no danger of dying out.

Revived by these verities, the driver hurries on to the particular town that is his chosen oasis for weekends and summer vacations. It may be quite near, if the town is Westhampton or Quogue. It may be almost an hour farther if the town is Southampton or Water Mill or Sag Harbor, and it will be still more if it is East Hampton, Amagansett, or Montauk Point itself, where the highway at last defers to the ocean. Long Island is more aptly named than most people think. The glamourous "Hamptons," bunched together in popular fancy, are actually scattered across thirty-five miles.

Nor is geography all that divides them and their satellite villages. In social structure and attitude they are as different as cummerbund and hula skirt, and each is a zealous guardian of its own codes of privacy and familiarity, dress and undress, tolerance and intolerance. Some have become cells for artists or writers or theatrical folk, and so have sprouted *chichi* shops on Main Street and glass houses in the surrounding fields. Others have tried to hold the line—to preserve their identity as bastions of the old guard—against the tide of new settlers. But the tide is getting bigger every year. To be far out on Long Island is now very much In.

Many of these towns, of course, have long been summer colonies, but distance kept them beyond common reach. Now, however, new expressways have abridged the miles,

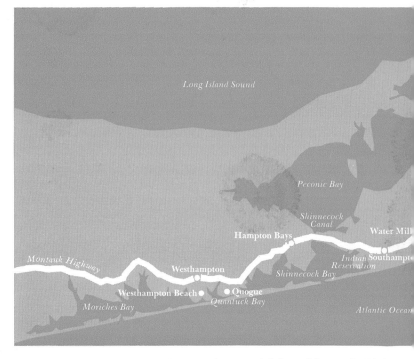

Two-lane and twisting, dodging bays and inlets, Montauk Highway

long weekends have created more leisure, and easy credit has enabled the city dweller to buy or rent a "second home." Once he finds this home, even if it is only a shack, he is its champion and slave.

Every Friday night, in a car distended with portable cribs, portable babies, and other familial gear, he leaves New York and hurtles to outer Long Island, drawn to his goal as obsessively as any pilgrim. On Sunday night, broiled by the sun, washed externally by the ocean and internally by gin, he bundles his cranky children into the car, hopeful that by starting early he will "beat the traffic," and turns his headlights westward for the long voyage home, one which doesn't beat the traffic and which never seems to end.

Such a trip, repeated so often, ought to blunt the strongest passion. Yet the call of outer Long Island continues to drown out the voices of logic and gloom. Those who keep answering the call, week after week, do so for different specific pleasures, but they are all joined in the belief that the area has a special feeling they would not find anywhere else.

Essentially it is a feeling of openness. The terrain is flat, and its most congenial crops are those that do not grow high enough to block the view. Potatoes are obviously the most congenial of all—potato fields, distinctively green, stretch away for miles, their linear pattern broken only by a random house or windmill. It is not a view for anyone who wants

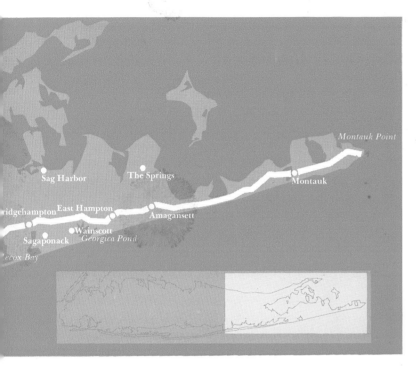

is the artery of summertime arts on Long Island's southern shore

his scenery to be spectacular. This is a landscape of subtle charms.

Yet many new settlers would rather build beside a potato field than beside a beach, and it is not hard to see why. A driver who turns off the Montauk Highway onto the smaller roads that interlace these fields will soon succumb to their repose and their austere beauty. Perhaps only the interior of New England has this Early American quality, and there no water enlarges the view.

On outer Long Island water is always near and often in sight. Sometimes it lies beyond a potato field: pale blue tacked onto pale green. It is not necessarily the ocean. Behind barriers of sand, the ocean has formed (and the Indians have largely named) Moriches Bay and Quantuck Bay, Shinnecock and Mecox and Peconic bays, and many other gentle bodies of water which are all things to all sportsmen —to the swift water-skier and the stuck clam-digger—and are equally kind to experts and beginners, old and young.

A boy learning to sail can own the water, and so can his sailboat-racing father who already knows how, and so can their natural enemy, the motorboatman, that urban admiral who goes from one marina to another on Saturday afternoon, playing cards on the deck as if he had never left home. Novice fishermen will catch as many snappers as the old

pro. Luck favors those who haven't particularly earned it, and this is all the assurance that the newcomer needs.

Hearing of the bounty of the bays, passing stores that sell marine equipment, seeing small boats being towed on trailers to the sea, he soon stops thinking of the water as alien territory. It becomes an extension of himself and of his attainable world. He buys a boat and begins going for rides as habitually as he used to take his family out in the car. He learns the release of putting out from land, symbol of his weekday woes, and looking back at it in tranquillity, briefly beyond the reach of bosses, bankers, relatives, headlines, unwashed dishes, and other mortal coils.

But of course it is the ocean that gives outer Long Island its true extra dimension. If oceans vary in beauty according to the shore that they meet, the Atlantic can hardly be more beautiful than it is here, for it breaks onto a smooth white beach that appears to have no limit in either direction. Though countless summer houses now perch on its dunes, though bathers swarm over it from June to September, they scarcely make a dent on the vast purity of the shoreline. Even people who live a few miles inland are subject to its elemental power. They do not like to let a day elapse without driving down to see and hear and smell the ocean, to savor its changing patterns and colors, and often, toward evening, they do.

If it is a violent ocean, so much the better—high winds make the sea, if anything, more hypnotic and beautiful. Outer Long Islanders have known many such seas in their hurricane-tossed lives. Their recent folklore abounds with storms named Carla and Donna and Ella, and the evidence is still strewn before their eyes—an icebox, perhaps, or a bathtub left naked on the sand by a wave that washed away the house which it was in.

One of these houses now sits in Moriches Bay, a memento of last year's storm that severed the Westhampton dune, and at least its whereabouts are known. Fifty others vanished completely, borne out of sight but not, needless to say, out of mind for the people who owned them. Here nobody forgets that the gods of wrath are still mightier than the gods of realty. A man whose house overlooks the beach may ostensibly have his eye on the steak that he is barbecuing, or on the bikini wiggling by. Actually his eye is on those dark clouds forming in the west.

Onto this natural playground the new settlers have grafted their playhouses in every conceivable and inconceivable shape. Their impact on some communities has been heavy; on others they make almost no mark. It depends on whether the town fathers want to save their original character or bend their zoning laws to catch the summer trade.

Nowhere have the invaders been embraced more avidly than in Westhampton. This is the nearest of the far-out colonies, and its beach is the most breathtaking. Consequently, unlike the farther-out towns which appeal to artists and writers who are in no great hurry, it attracts the feverish folk of Broadway, movies, television, advertising, and publicity. As speed is their mainspring and sun-worship their summer religion, they find Westhampton ideal for its proximity and climate. Quitting work on Friday night, they hop into their sports cars—curled beside them are the ladies with whom they will be spending the weekend, who quite often are their wives—and roar out from Manhattan to the houses that they have built on Dune Road.

These houses, quite close together, appear to sit in mid-air. They are on stilts, theoretically safe from high seas that might crash over the dune, and each is a novel projection of ramps and decks which enable the owner to bask in the sun all day, clad in a bathing suit, playing Scrabble and listening to LP's of Broadway shows, without going near the water. Along this road a half-dozen huge hotels, "boatels," night clubs, and co-operative apartments have also been allowed to rise, ugly leviathans that dwarf their simpler surroundings.

Traffic, as a result, is fast and fierce, day and night, as the beach dwellers go to each other's houses for parties or into the village for provisions. The village of Westhampton Beach, ordinarily small and sleepy, turns in summer into a miniature Miami, a continuing display of beachwear in all the colors of the rainbow and many more. Fey little art galleries and specialty shops bloom for three months between the butcher, the plumber, the electrician, and the general store, patronized by women in cerise toreador pants, high-heeled sandals, and sequined dark glasses of enormous size —acquaintances in New York but unrecognized by each other in all this casual panoply. Radios blare out of open Jaguars, and the talk on the sidewalk is of "picture deals" and box-office grosses. In various pockets of the village the old residents retain their oases—their country club, beach clubs, and staid houses—but it is not the same place where they first planted their flag and sank their spiked golf shoes a generation or two ago.

The adjoining village of Quogue, by contrast, recently celebrated its three-hundredth year and still looks like that kind of town. Its wide and tree-lined main street is as serene as Westhampton's is not, and along its side roads are dozens of brown-shingled houses, big and roomy and ringed with porches, that uniquely spell "summer colony" in the American East. If Quogue lacks the vitality of its neighbor, it has a compensating beauty and peace. And if a deep peace has also settled over its ideas and opinions, that is the price which such dynastic resorts pay—and are glad to pay—for stability in a time of change.

No Long Island resort is as dynastic, however, as Southampton, a half hour farther on, beyond Hampton Bays and the Shinnecock Canal (which the Indians called "Canoe Place" and which is still thick with boats), and beyond the little reservation where a few Indians still live and hold an annual powwow. These Shinnecocks are obviously the first families of Southampton, though the English made a good run for getting there early, as their clapboard houses, dating from the mid sixteen-hundreds, attest.

But it is the current families who give the impression of having owned the town forever. Their big and pretentious mansions exude the very essence of accumulated wealth— they are set on vast estates, approached by long driveways, guarded by ornate portals, and encircled by hedges so impeccably trimmed that their care must occupy the entire corps of local laborers from May to October. There is something forlorn about these stone palaces that trail off into servants' wings for servants who no longer exist, immense ghosts from the age of Gatsby, outmoded by time and taxes.

Their owners nevertheless continue to fight the good fight. Lawn tennis is still maintained in the grand manner at the Meadow Club; the patriarchal Bathing Corporation is still the sole answer to that curious question, "Where do you bathe?" and the after-dark amusements, judging by the local newspaper columns, still invoke the desperate gaiety of the Jazz Age.

When the Southampton folk emerge from their various warrens, it is usually to go shopping and rub elbows of bright silk and cashmere in Job's Lane. This short street manages to compress many of America's most expensive clothing salons, antique dealers, and other sellers of elegant baubles. Only a few yards away, by coincidence, is the Southampton historical museum, which contains some of America's oldest, rudest, and most utilitarian objects. Thus the genteel millionaire also rubs elbows with his fibrous ancestor—an encounter not to be missed.

It is because Southampton is such a cul-de-sac that the new settlers have pushed right past it to the wide, open potato fields, uncluttered dunes, and liberal winds of Water Mill, Bridgehampton, and Sagaponack. The very openness of this region is its best defense against conformity. The houses are dispersed widely, wherever a city dweller has been able to buy a few acres from a potato farmer, and they are as different as their owners. Some are old barns which artists have converted to their use; some are new geometric forms, mostly of glass, which architects have raised for themselves and their venturesome clients.

To call this area an artists' "colony" is not strictly true. It is not compact enough. Nevertheless a growing number of artists, musicians, writers, and editors live here, and anyone who wants to talk shop will find his man within ten miles —or his woman, for many of these marriages were made, if not necessarily in heaven, at least on Parnassus. The composer composes while his wife paints, and when the literary critic takes a wife she is often a lady novelist.

In only one of the far-out towns are the new settlers wholly invisible: Sag Harbor. Quite a few artists and writers have bought houses in this old whaling port, but it is clear that they chose the town for what it was and not for what they could make it into. Its main street is the most purely American, with a red-brick municipal hall built in 1846, and it has not changed much since the days that are glorified in its whaling museum. It has no chic shops, and as one artist said, "Nobody would use them if it did."

Still farther on, the Montauk Highway turns abruptly into one of America's prettiest towns. At first glance the spacious main street of East Hampton, divided by a broad common and a pond, flanked by historic houses, terminating in an ancient windmill, looks almost "restored." All, however, is genuine; the village has simply kept the shape that its original settlers fixed in 1648.

Newer settlers have long been lured by its charm and its fine ocean beach, and as these "summer people" were mainly members of the old guard, they have made East Hampton into the most posh of the far-out towns. Their houses have the studied simplicity of the aristocratic rich. Their club, the Maidstone, a monolith of golf courses, swimming pools, beach cabanas, ballrooms, and bars, sits on a hill like a Tudor manor and dominates the residential section in more ways than one. East Hampton society falls into two distinct groups: those who belong to Maidstone, and all the rest.

As this is not the chummiest arrangement, the very new settlers—particularly those of creative bent—have fanned out to nearby villages of less formality, where Bermuda shorts are not a required uniform, such as Amagansett, or have staked out local beaches of their own. The busiest of

these, the "Coast Guard Beach," is popular with theatrical producers and playwrights. In fact, a faithful reader of the Broadway columns is led to believe that half the shows in any season originate when Producer X, emerging from the surf, spots Songwriter Y under an umbrella, recognizes Dramatist Z coming over the dunes with his crossword puzzle, sees Director A playing volleyball with Ingénue B, and signs them all to do a musical that has just occurred to him, with the help of Lady Agent C, who pops providentially out of the sand at that very moment.

Only one far-out town is really an "artists' colony"—an odd little settlement three miles out of East Hampton called The Springs—and it is not a town at all. Served only by a tiny grocery store and a gas pump, it consists of a lonely road that wanders through field and scrub with sporadic houses on either side. They are nondescript old farmhouses, and nobody would suspect that they now belong to important artists, who have kept the plain exteriors and streamlined the rooms inside.

Jackson Pollock, fleeing the hostile New York art world, came to this isolated spot in 1946, and gradually other painters followed. As Pollock's work at last caught on, and especially after his death in 1956, the colony became almost a shrine, and so did the Pollock house where his widow, Lee Krasner, still lives and paints. Today the abstract expressionists in The Springs form a sizable clique, and they do not lack for admirers—East Hampton is full of wealthy patrons and hangers-on who love to give twist parties for the painters and thereby crash their world.

"After a while," one young artist says, "some of these party givers start painting—and then of course we drop them."

Having no beach of their own, the artists of The Springs use the Coast Guard Beach in East Hampton, but not for inspiration—unlike the other creative folk who have settled in Long Island's far-out towns in the hope that the wild beauty of the landscape will have a beneficial influence on their work. "We bring our image out from New York," says one abstract expressionist, "and that's what we paint. The other day a group of us were down at the beach, talking, when a lady came along with a paintbox, and do you know she had the audacity to sit down and paint the ocean."

So heavily do the city dwellers imprint themselves on the rural landscape during June, July, and August that it is hard to conceive of a time when they will go away again. Summer's lease, Shakespeare notwithstanding, has all too long a date—or so the serious artists of the region would say. They can hardly wait for the Labor Day weekend, after which most leases expire and they are left, at last, in peace.

On the day after Labor Day they awaken to a quiet that is almost primordial. The last transistor radio has gone crooning back to Manhattan, and not a single Jaguar remains to terrorize the roads. The local news dealer has stopped selling *Variety*; talk has consequently shifted from the turkeys of faraway Broadway to the ducks of the farmer next door. The Long Island Railroad's daily "Cannonball," a faithful if somewhat misnamed train that has been a rolling house party all summer long, bringing out from New York every Friday afternoon a steamy tangle of seersucker coats, cotton dresses, and new-strung tennis rackets, is back to normal length and personality, shorn of the extra parlor cars that the line adds in warm weather to coddle, or at least anesthetize, its richer riders.

Even nature conspires to set the day after Labor Day apart from all others. By coincidence, or perhaps by some mystical law, it is invariably a day of such clarity as to wash the land clean and announce its renewal. Outer Long Islanders boast that autumn, not spring, is the best time of year; and they are right. There is a pinch in the air and a brilliance in the sky, and the water is of a blue so pale that it almost ceases to be blue. Anyone who walks on the beach, now swept of summer's traces, will share it only with the birds stopping off on their southward flight; it is as near to solitude and serenity as many people manage to come.

This is when the various artists of far-out Long Island, staying on, really get down to work, when presumably their muses are most propitious. The novelist writes with fresh vitality, the critic's vision is as clear as the atmosphere around him. The poet's well of imagery, brackish all summer, is suddenly replenished and pure. The composer hears no dissonant note, and even the abstract painter, who claims immunity to his environment, sees taking shape on his canvas a pattern whose tensions are less tense than usual.

If this is not necessarily a good thing, if these are currents that the artists do not want to see in their art, they can repair the damage overnight by returning to the anxious city. With every year, however, they seem less and less impelled to do so, which would suggest that in their gradual colonization of this spacious land they have found—and founded—a real "artists' colony" after all.

William K. Zinsser spends his summers in the Hamptons and his winters in New York, and writes in—and about—both places. His most recent book is called The City Dwellers.

Eli Wallach and Anne Jackson

East Hampton, long a market town for Long Island farmers and a haven for the rich, has lately acquired a summer theatrical community; and the Wallachs, who come here with their three children, count a clutch of New York producers and directors among their neighbors: Kermit Bloomgarden, Fred Coe, Arthur Cantor, André Gregory, David Ross. Mr. and Mrs. Wallach, two of the most distinguished and versatile members of The Actors Studio, make for this quiet town, with its village green, its duckpond, and its elms, whenever they are not performing elsewhere; last year they put on a program of readings in East Hampton's John Drew Theatre. They have also appeared together on Broadway (*Major Barbara* and *Rhinoceros*), on tour (*The Glass Menagerie*), and off Broadway this past season in two plays, *The Typists* and *The Tiger*, as well as separately on stage, screen, and uncounted television shows. Late last summer Wallach was in Europe on the set of Carl Foreman's new movie, *The Victors;* this season he and Miss Jackson hope to spend most of their time on East Hampton's bleached sands.

PHOTOGRAPHED FOR HORIZON BY HANS NAMUTH

Gwen Verdon

The modest beach house occupied by one of Broadway's most ebullient, attractive performers and her husband, the choreographer-director Bob Fosse, was originally part of an Army quarantine camp built at Montauk Point during the Spanish-American war. Later it was moved to its present location near Amagansett, where the Fosses found and bought it four years ago. They use it all year as a weekend retreat from their city schedules, which include—for Miss Verdon—continued study. She began ballet lessons when she was five and has always, she says, "thought of myself as being primarily a dancer"; but she also won several acting awards in 1953 for her first important role, in *Can-Can*. She added singing to her professional accomplishments in *Damn Yankees!*, *New Girl in Town*, and the musical especially written for her, *Redhead*. Here she faces the ocean in front of a tangle of brush and fencing, meant to anchor the dune against the Atlantic storms. Miss Verdon likes to make collages for her living room from driftwood, bits of broken glass, and other beach-combing discoveries.

Saul Steinberg

Five years have passed since the artist Saul Steinberg moved into his awkward, dark-shingled, peak-roofed house in The Springs, near East Hampton (the former owner was the keeper of the Montauk lighthouse), and he has added to it only the creosote-colored studio seen over his shoulder. Steinberg's drawings (now that museums collect them they can hardly be called "cartoons") appear mainly in *The New Yorker* and in his books, the last of which (a selection from the previous three) he called *The Catalogue*. Steinberg's world of visual puns extends to the interior of his house, sparsely furnished and underdecorated, the better to set off objects he has liked and acquired —an old-fashioned stained-glass lampshade, a hideously fascinating tinted photograph of a coy girl under convex glass. Having lived in cities most of his life (Bucharest, Milan, Santo Domingo, New York), he is becoming a convert to the delights of country living. "Other people are doing it," he says. "My generation, anyway. You slowly discover sunsets and birds. Of course, the birds made me nervous at first."

Gordon Bunshaft

It is somewhat to his own surprise that the architect Gordon Bunshaft finds himself the owner of a new house being built on Georgica Pond near East Hampton. He is a partner and chief designer in the New York office of Skidmore, Owings & Merrill, and is generally credited with such SOM landmarks as Lever House in New York and the Connecticut General Life Insurance Company's headquarters near Hartford. But he had never designed a building for himself—despite the fact that he and his wife have been vacationing on Long Island for a dozen years—until about a year ago when he and Edward J. Mathews (another SOM partner) became concerned about a developer's plans for some land close to a plot that Mathews occupies. One thing led to another, and Bunshaft ended up with two acres on a wooded point. Here he is putting up a concrete and marble "box," very long and low, which he describes as "more like an Italian villa" than the usual East Hampton dwelling. He and his wife, Nina, have collaborated on designing the house.

David Oppenheim

One of the most accomplished clarinetists playing today—he appears regularly with the Budapest Quartet—David Oppenheim commutes diligently during the summer to the clean air and open country of Water Mill. The house he rents for his family faces a flat potato field, beyond which lies the grandiose estate of Henry Ford II and, beyond that, the ocean. This location is conveniently near the homes of such friends as the duo-pianists Gold and Fizdale, and the painter Jane Wilson and her husband, John Gruen. Seated in the stranded dory that is his children's playpen, he practices trills and scales for his daughter Sarah, five, and—in the background—his wife, Ellen, and four-year-old son, Tommy; but he does this only rarely. A restless, genial man, Oppenheim has resolutely divided his career between music and other activities: he has been head of the classical music division of Columbia Records, a television producer, and is now moving into the theatre; his first venture will be as a coproducer of Saul Bellow's play *The Upper Depths* next season.

FAR OUT ON LONG ISLAND (CONTINUED)

16

Marya Mannes

The summer house in Sagaponack belonging to the author Marya Mannes and her husband, Christoper Clarkson, is enclosed by dense hedges. But if the Clarksons cherish the privacy of their "escape hatch," they also like to walk the beach, picking up abandoned toys to mount on their tool-shed door or strange shells for the house ("but we don't make lampshades of anything"). The air here is full of salt, but no more so than Miss Mannes's writing. From her verse and essays in *The Reporter* she has assembled two volumes, *Subverse: Rhymes for Our Times* and *More in Anger: Some Opinions Uncensored and Unteleprompted*. The latter reaches all across the landscape of modern culture to jab at hypocrisy here or commercialism there, and it has established Marya Mannes as satire's first lady.

Peter Blake

Peter Blake's summer home at Bridgehampton looks out across a watery view of Mecox Bay. Blake—an architect, writer, and editor—was among the first to build a modern house at Long Island's far end. He has since sold it and built the one above, which is also of his own design: two connected pavilions, one for living, one for sleeping. He is German-born and came to this country in 1939. For a time he was curator of architecture at the Museum of Modern Art; then he joined the staff of *Architectural Forum*, of which he is now managing editor. In 1958 he opened his own architectural office (with Julian Neski) and has designed some dozen houses in the Bridgehampton neighborhood, as well as elsewhere. Balloons are not ordinarily part of the décor; it was his son's birthday.

17

Charles Addams

Unable to buy an eccentric-looking billiard house that looms out of a Westhampton back yard, Charles Addams, of *New Yorker* fame, had it copied (with a few improvements) when he built this studio beside the channel that connects Moriches and Quantuck bays. There he goes in summer and on winter weekends, usually driving back and forth from his New York apartment in an Alfa Romeo rather than the 1925 Bugatti seen here under his elbow (Addams keeps the Bugatti in trim for the vintage car races held each fall at Bridgehampton). He has been coming to Westhampton Beach for eleven years, and is a familiar figure along Dune Road. Relaxing in sport shirt, espadrilles, and corduroy trousers, he seems far removed from the mood of his macabre cartoons. Only one genuinely Addams touch is evident in his *ambiance* here: the ground around his studio is alive with poison ivy.

Jane Wilson

The prettiest painter on Long Island (and one of the best) lives beside a potato field with her husband, the composer and critic John Gruen. In Water Mill and nearby are many good friends: the painter Jane Freilicher and her husband, the Oppenheims, Gold and Fizdale, Larry Rivers. Although she has worked as a fashion model on occasion, ever since she studied art at the University of Iowa Miss Wilson has never thought of herself as anything but a painter. Her studio is the attic, and she works there in the mornings when not busy with her four-year-old daughter or household duties. What she likes about the area is its Dutch quality of flatness and openness, with farms beside the sea ("fertility goes right up to the ocean"). All this is reflected in the fresh and freehand character of the semi-imaginary, semi-abstract landscapes for which she is now widely known.

From the balcony that surrounds the second story of his house, Mediterranean-style, Montoya can look out across Georgica Pond in one direction and across an inlet to the ocean beach in another (sometimes, as here, there is nothing to be seen in any direction). Born in Madrid, he is *gitano por los cuatros costados*—gypsy on all four sides—and he "grew up playing the guitar," although his real intention was to become a civil servant. But then he had a chance to play in the troupe of the famous flamenco dancer "La Argentina," and left bureaucracy forever. Since 1945 he has been giving solo recitals on the concert stage, with his wife—herself an exponent of the Spanish dance—as his personal manager. From his fingers flamenco guitar music sounds as intricate as a contrapuntal melody of Bach in Segovia's hands, yet there is always an element of improvisation: no two performances are identical. Flamenco is, in this sense, like jazz, and to prove it Montoya has teamed up with a rhythm section to record his versions of "St. Louis Blues" and "Blues in the Night."

A. J. Liebling and Jean Stafford

The atmosphere, homes, and accents of outer Long Island remind Liebling of those of rural New England. His own house is an example: two-storied, faced with weathered shingles, and at one time surrounded by a forty-acre poultry farm. Here the Lieblings while away their summer days trying not to work—that is, write. Miss Stafford, the author of numerous short stories and several novels *(Boston Adventure, The Mountain Lion, The Catherine Wheel)*, sits under an apple tree with some petit-point embroidery and tries to warn the birds away from her cat, the eponymous hero of her children's book *Elephi, the Cat with the High I.Q.* Liebling clips hedges. At other times he is the conscience of American journalism (in his studies in *The New Yorker* of "The Wayward Press") and an authority on boxing and eating. In his latest book, *Between Meals*, succulent reminiscences are interlarded—to use a term that began in the kitchen—with warnings against "the ulcers that come from worrying about a balanced diet" and being seduced by "the fatal trap of abstinence."

Lee Krasner

The widow of Jackson Pollock now uses his studio for her own work (her old one, off in the woods, has been converted into a cottage). The two painters moved out to The Springs in 1946 and lived there, summer and winter, until Pollock's death ten years later. Since then Miss Krasner has been spending the winter months in town, but summer finds her hard at work in the big studio with its excellent light and undistracting simplicity (there is not even a spigot: she brings water out from the house in sprinkling cans). Although her style was undoubtedly influenced by her late husband's innovations and theories, it is quite distinctly her own. Under the window are some recent experiments in crayon and chalk, sketches only, and on the other wall are two finished oils dating from 1958 and 1960. Anything but Bohemian, Miss Krasner has her clothes made by America's most cerebral couturier, Charles James, and her house is tasteful and feminine. It is filled with her own paintings, but there are no longer any Pollocks—they have become too precious and costly for a summer house.

Helen MacInnes and Gilbert Highet

The daily routine in East Hampton of the writing Highets usually includes nine holes of golf at the Maidstone Club, some swimming or gardening, and a game of chess. This is hardly the hedonistic existence one associates with such polished resorts, and it is not meant to be: for them, East Hampton is simply a pleasanter place to work in summer than the city. Much of their day is spent at two desks in the study, hers facing a view of the garden, his facing a bookcase filled with reference works. Miss MacInnes writes novels of suspense (a new one, *The Venetian Affair,* is to come out this fall); her husband, who is Anthon Professor of Latin at Columbia University, writes essays and books of criticism. They were both born in Glasgow and retain its characteristic burr in their speech, although they have lived in America since 1937. They have also retained a British taste in gardens; theirs is among the best-groomed in East Hampton, and the only one that domiciles a catbird trained to come when called and catch grapes in his beak. (Miss MacInnes, by the way, lost the game.)

Alexander Brook

The man with the 1915 Model T and the 1804 three-story house is one of America's best-established painters, although he had no exhibitions between 1950 and 1960. These were the years of the abstract expressionist interregnum, and he may have felt that his carefully painted nudes, landscapes, and still lifes would be ignored in the brouhaha over splash, splatter, and drip. But he went right on painting them, and now they are being recognized for what they are: works of consummate but unobtrusive craftsmanship that are as likely to endure as those of any other living American. Brook lives year-round in this house, which is just across a bridge from the main street of Sag Harbor and overlooks a wide stretch of busy, boat-flecked Shelter Island Sound. Off to the left is a former stable which now houses, besides the Model T, a 1935 Rolls-Royce and studios for himself and his wife, Gina Knee, also a painter. The two old cars are in perfect working order, and Brook enjoys driving them now and then for pleasure, but for his mundane errands he uses a station wagon of more recent date.

Costantino Nivola

Other artists may draw on the far-out Long Island landscape for inspiration or subject matter, but Costantino Nivola is the only one who has ever *used* it. Literally. Some years ago he developed a technique of carving forms in negative in the damp sand of the beach and casting them, then and there, in plaster. Endlessly inventive, born in Sardinia, and trained as a stone-mason (hence his easy authority with cement and concrete), Nivola was at twenty-five the art director of the Olivetti Company. Three years later, in 1939, he came to the United States. His first big sculpture project here was a relief mural for the Olivetti showroom in New York; his most recent is forty-five sculptures for the new Saarinen-designed colleges at Yale, carved on the spot in wet concrete. He is fond of Sardinia, where he had this corduroy suit made by a home-town tailor. But he is also fond of his house and forty acres in The Springs, where he has improved the scenery with outdoor murals and this fountain that teases the water down an aerial stairway.

Edward D. Stone

The man who is best known for making modern architecture sumptuous as well as functional spends his summer weekends in a house not noticeably qualified for either of these adjectives. It is old, plain, and of such daunting size (twenty-one rooms) that real-estate agents used to call it "The Stepchild," despite the fact that Jacqueline Kennedy spent her summers in it until she was fifteen. Stone bought it because he wanted a house by the sea for his wife and two small children. He is planning to wrap two balconies around it, with wider decks at the best vantage points, and to combine some of the rooms. But all this remains in abeyance until next fall, while he attends to his other far-flung activities. They include designing a nuclear institute in Pakistan, a new state Capitol for North Carolina, a trade center in New Orleans, the National Cultural Center in Washington, and various urban development projects that permit him to express his abhorrence of the automobile by keeping it, as far as possible, underground—out of the streets and out of sight.

CAN THIS DRUG ENLARGE MAN'S MIND ?

Narcotics numb it. Alcohol unsettles it.

Now a new chemical called LSD

has emerged with phenomenal powers

of intensifying and changing it—

whether for good or ill is a subject of hot debate

By GERALD HEARD

Since earliest times man has felt impulses to rise above his everyday self and achieve either some higher insight or some release from mundane concerns—or both. Western saints and Eastern mystics have subjected themselves to strenuous spiritual exercises; others, less dedicated, have resorted to chemical aids, from the ceremonial wine of the ancients and the opiates of the Orient to the sacramental peyotl plant of Aztec tribes and the social stimulants of our own day.

In our time, moreover, psychologists and other students of human perceptions, from William James to Aldous Huxley, have tried out on themselves certain experimental drugs in an effort to induce states that would lend extraordinary lucidity and light to the mind's unconscious and creative processes—possibly even assistance to these. Today these newer drugs— mescaline, psilocybin, and the latest and most potent of them, Lysergic Acid Diethylamide, or LSD—are spreading so widely on a "research" basis that major questions are arising as to their effects and proper use.

Their enemies call them "mind-distorting" drugs, and warn that their therapeutic values are unproven, that they may upset even a normal person, and that they are already being abused for "kicks." Their proponents prefer to call them "consciousness-changing" agents, and argue that in selected cases, for individuals of strong mental and creative powers, LSD may widen their window on the world and on themselves as well. On the evidence so far, both sides seem agreed that LSD is not habit-forming; numerous takers of it report that the experience is a strenuous and exhausting one, to be repeated only after much thought.

Should man in any case put such a potentially dangerous substance into his system? It is claimed for LSD that it is far less toxic than alcohol, tobacco, or caffeine. At the same time one of its leading students and advocates, Dr. Sidney Cohen (see also his statement on page 31), remarks: "It is quite possible that LSD attracts certain unstable individuals in their search for some magical intervention." Can trance-like insight produced by chemicals be the source of higher wisdom and creativity, like a kind of Instant Zen? This remains unproven—especially since so many persons coming back from LSD can describe their experience only as indescribable.

One of those who can describe it best is the writer of the following article, the distinguished philosopher Gerald Heard, author of The Eternal Gospel, The Doppelgangers, Is God in History?, *and other books, and a leading student of psychic research. Comments by some other authorities expressing divergent opinions on the LSD issue are presented beside his text.*

What will men of the future consider the greatest achievements of our time? Releasing hydrogen energy? Putting a man on the moon? Extending the average human life to a century or more?

Last year Dr. Glenn T. Seaborg, Chairman of the United States Atomic Energy Commission, gave his forecast of what he thought might be our most revolutionary discoveries or advances in the next generation. Addressing the graduating class of Northern Michigan College in his home state, he asked his listeners to project themselves forward to their thirtieth reunion in 1992, and selected fifteen items on which to speculate. Fourteen of these—ranging from the realizing of space communications to capturing solar energy and the remaking of daily life by electronic computers—dealt with physical advances, and thus with the same objective that Francis Bacon had put before the pristine scientists of ten generations ago: "the relief of man's estate." The fifteenth, however, would not have occurred to Elizabethan England's "wide-browed Verulam," or indeed to any researcher until the last dozen years.

"Pharmaceuticals that change and maintain human personality at any desired level," was Dr. Seaborg's definition of this major new possibility of power—and, he was quick to add, of potential danger too. He was thinking of such recently introduced drugs as mescaline, psilocybin, and no doubt particularly of the phenomenal one known as LSD, about the uses of which much controversy is raging today. Of them he went on to say: "It may . . . become necessary to establish new legal and moral codes to govern those who prescribe use of these materials. Who should prescribe . . . and under what conditions, such a drug to a person in a position of high authority when he is faced with decisions of great consequence?"

Of course man has had mood-changing drugs at his disposal for millennia. First came alcohol, the great relaxant; then opium, the painkiller; then caffeine, the spur of the nervous system; then cocaine, hashish, and a score of other less common vegetable extracts. And in the last few years a wide variety of tranquilizers has been developed.

They all, however, fall into one or the other of two classes. They either weaken the mind's common-sense grasp of things, as does alcohol or opium, or they strengthen that grip, as does coffee or dexedrine. They do not leave the mind unclouded and yet at the same time permit it to view things in quite an uncommonsensical way. They do not raise the mind to high lucidity and yet at the same time make the world it views appear fraught with an intensity of significance that everyday common sense cannot perceive.

In LSD, or Lysergic Acid Diethylamide, however, a drug now exists that can accomplish all these aims. As Dr. Seaborg and several medical authorities cited in these pages emphasize, it is certainly not to be taken lightly, and research has only begun on its possibilities as a therapeutic aid in psychiatry. For many who have taken it under proper, controlled conditions, it has brought about an astonishing enlargement of sensitivity and perceptiveness, and it may thus cast new light on the wellsprings of creativity.

If you ask, Of what possible use is such a drug? or, What is the difference between the effects of taking LSD and, say, hashish in a Tangier dive or opium in Hong Kong? the answer might be given in terms of an early Franciscan, the ex-lawyer Jacoponi da Todi, when asked the same "what's the use" question after he spoke of the exhilarating effect that joining Saint Francis's company had on him. His response was, "a better order in all my living."

Not an opiate or a narcotic, LSD is a chemical able to produce profound changes of consciousness which, in healthily constituted persons, seem to leave no untoward aftereffects. And while it can give an ecstatic experience, at the same time it lends an extraordinary intensity of attention.

You see and hear this world, but as the artist and the musician sees and hears. And, much more important, it may also give far-reaching insights into one's own self and into one's relationship with others. Some takers of it have even felt that they had won an insight into the "nature of the Universe and the purpose of Life." These insights can be remembered and, if the person wishes, can be incorporated into his or her everyday living to bring it a "better order."

So here may be a major breakthrough that meets the problem of letting in a free flow of comprehension beyond the everyday threshold of experience while keeping the mind clear. And this seems to be accomplished by a confronting of one's self, a standing outside one's self, a dissolution of the ego-based apprehensions that cloud the sky of the mind.

The drug was discovered by accident in 1943. Dr. Albert Hofmann of Sandoz Ltd. in Switzerland, while doing research with derivatives of the ergot alkaloids, somehow absorbed synthesized LSD into his system and found it to have surprising effects on consciousness. It was soon recognized as the most potent and reliable of the consciousness-changing drugs. A remarkable fact about it is the extreme minuteness of the effective dose. The optimum dosage—that which produces for the subject the most informative results —lies between 100 and 150 "gamma"; and 100 "gamma" is approximately one ten-thousandth of a gram. (Mescaline, another of the "consciousness-changers," has to be taken in a dosage four thousand times that of LSD to produce similar mental results, and in this amount it does have physical effects on most subjects—sometimes unpleasant ones.)

A good psychiatrist, of course, must be the overseer of all LSD research. He must, as did the physicians who trained the volunteers for the ascent of

Mount Everest, have "vetted" the subject. He must know whether this or that particular psyche is likely to function satisfactorily at these rare altitudes. Then, a person intimately acquainted with LSD should be at the side of the subject as he embarks on his journey. It should not be undertaken alone. A companion should be on call to act as an assistant—for instance, to play music, change the lighting, answer any questions, or write down any remarks the subject should wish recorded—and also as a monitor, or night watchman, so to speak, ready to report if possible trouble may be lurking ahead (in which case the voyage can be called off instantly by administering a counteracting chemical).

So, though the subject should not be intruded upon, he should not be left figuratively or literally in the dark. The optimal circumstances are simple, though contrary to present clinical and laboratory protocol. For the ideal setting is not a hospital or research lab, but rather an environment that is neither aggressive nor austere, and in which he may feel at home, perhaps a quiet house surrounded by a garden.

The first stage under LSD is surprising in a paradoxical way. From what he has learned about this research, the subject is of course expecting a surprise. But during the first hour after swallowing the tiny pills, he usually experiences nothing at all. He may feel some relief at finding himself remaining completely normal, and perhaps a secret sense of superiority at the thought that possibly he is too strong to give in to a drug that will take him away from reality. An uncommonly able businessman, the head of a major corporation, who had much wished to take LSD, in fact waited fully three and one half hours for something to "happen." Although it is uncommon for LSD to be so long in taking effect, the occasions on which this has occurred have led some researchers to speculate that the onset of the experience can be held at bay for an extra hour or two by the subject's unconscious nervousness or his suspicion that he might have been given nothing more than an innocuous placebo.

Yet as the first hour wears away, quite a number of subjects become convinced that they are feeling odd. Some, like the witches of *Macbeth,* feel a pricking in their thumbs. Others—and this, too, is a common reaction to the weird, the uncanny, the "numinous"—feel chill, with that tightening, or horripilation, of the skin as, in the vernacular, "a goose goes over one's grave." They report, "I am trembling"—but, putting out their hands, find them steady.

In the second hour, however, most subjects enter upon a stage which can leave no doubt that a profound change of consciousness is occurring. For one thing, the attending psychiatrist, or "sitter," can see that the pupils of the subject's eyes are now nearly always dilated. This symptom is the first and often the only undeniable and visible physical effect of LSD, and it gives the physiologist almost his only clue as to which area of the brain is now being acted upon. For the center that controls the pupils' reaction to light is known, and it lies deep.

During this second hour we can say that the subject is "gaining altitude." How does he record this heightening of consciousness? By far the most common remark refers to the growing intensification of color. Flowers, leaves, grass, trees, are seen with tremendous vividness—"with the intensity that Van Gogh must have seen them," is an often-used description. They seem to pulse and breathe; in fact, even everyday, fixed objects around the room may take on "flowing," "waving" shapes, as if invested with some life force of their own. Intensification of sounds, too (such as the singing of birds, though far away), is often commented on with fascinated surprise. Music frequently becomes an absorbing delight even to the nonmusical—while to the musical it has on occasion become almost unbearably intense. "Under LSD I asked that my favorite recording of my favorite Beethoven quartet (Opus 135) be played," one musical taker reported; "but after a few minutes I had it turned off. Its emotions had become too searing—and besides, I had suddenly made the discovery that one of the instruments was playing ever so slightly off pitch."

Another effect is stranger and deeper. The subject feels that time itself—time urgent, pressing, hurried, or contrariwise, time slack, lagging, heavy on his hands—is now in "right time." When he discovers what an ample store of unhastened attention he can give to all the rich content brought him by eye and ear, he finds it hard not to believe that somehow time has been stretched. But a glance at his watch tells him it is a new-given power of superattention that is allowing him to make such full use of every moment.

It is, however, in the next couple of hours that for most people the full power of the experience comes over them. Till then, however absorbed, the subject has still been an observer. Now, although sights and sounds, the artistic splendor of the world, and the magic of music may still amaze him, they are, as it were, the décor, the scenery of a drama. Now the whole outside world becomes a composition that embraces and interfuses everything. And yet this composition, though constantly changing, is also (strange paradox) all the while complete and instant in a fathomless peace. At this point one could say that he crosses a watershed. In this all-pervading Energy he feels around him, the subject realizes that he cannot be isolated. It is flowing through him, as it flows through all that surrounds him.

Here his experience with time goes still further.

Time appears to have stopped, disappeared. What has now befallen the "voyager" is not merely that he is on the high seas with his ship in a vast calm, but that the ship itself no longer seems distinct from the infinite ocean. He stands outside of and apart from his familiar ego, all its protective barriers having been shed; and this can lead in some to transcendent experience, while in others to a deep panic. To those for whom their ego is their only possible self, the only possible mode of consciousness, its disappearance is a kind of death.

It is here that the subject, however independent-minded, may literally welcome a helping hand. Of all the senses, touch is naturally most firmly anchored in the material world. So it is the least liable to illusions. It has been found that if at the moment of this "transvaluation of all values," this double change of the view of one's self and one's view of nature, a hand is actually held out to the subject, he will be able to keep his bearings. If the subject uses this simple "sea anchor," he may discover that he is not merely "riding the swell" but has entered a condition of what until then may have been inconceivable. With his consciousness enlarged out of all bounds, he may—if all goes well—find that he no longer feels anxiety about past or future.

It is not that he has gone into amnesia. He can clearly recall past concerns and future appointments; but he recalls them as a wise guardian carries in his mind the affairs of his ward. His personal appetites, meanwhile, generally become suspended. Most people never eat or drink during the experience, though it may last a full day; even constant smokers, while they may start with a cigarette, put it down as soon as they begin to "climb." There is not the slightest repugnance to food and drink. It is simply that the subject feels the appetites are irrelevant. Any sexual sensation, any erotic fantasy or preoccupation, is nearly always reported as absent. So, for all its liberating powers, LSD remains noneuphoric: as the Greeks would say, it is "eudaemonic"—"a possession by the spirit of wholeness."

After these climactic hours, during which he may either have sat still and wordless while contemplating the myriad images borne in on him, or conveyed volubly to his companion or monitor what he has seen and felt, the voyager returns gradually to shore, sometimes dipping back into the tides of the far sea until the lingering powers of the chemical disperse.

In the *Odyssey* Penelope, the first hostess in recorded history, gives what one might call the first psychoanalytic interpretation of a dream. The returning Ulysses, appearing in disguise and keeping his identity concealed from her after his ten years' absence, questions her about a dream she has had concerning the fate of her exigent suitors. She answers:

CONTINUED ON PAGE 114

LSD in California: at Odds

Pro. A statement made to HORIZON by Sidney Cohen, M.D., Chief of Psychosomatic Medicine, Veterans Administration Center, Los Angeles; editor of MIND: Psychiatry in General Practice, and a pioneer in studies of the drug:

Considering the enormous scope of the psychic responses it induces, LSD is an astonishingly safe drug. One might have predicted that an agent that can bring about profound alterations of self-concept and an upsurge of repressed guilt-laden memories could leave its imbibers in a chaotic emotional state. We have administered LSD thousands of times to hundreds of people under a great variety of situations, and from our experience can say that except in rare instances, this does not occur. It was when an individual was verging on a "break," however, or when the investigator handled him unskillfully, that the rare instances of prolonged ill effects have occurred.

To take LSD for frivolous reasons, under unsupervised conditions where countermeasures are unavailable, can be dangerous. The drug is not so safe that it is something for everybody, but in a proper setting it can be something for some bodies. It does not cause addiction as opiates do, it does not produce physical and social disabilities as does alcohol, but it can certainly "fragment" a borderline individual. All good things can and will, unhappily, be used for harm.

Con. From a statement "Concerning the Use of Lysergic Acid Diethylamide" issued by the Council of the Southern California Psychiatric Society:

Lysergic Acid Diethylamide, as an adjunct to psychotherapy, has been hailed in sensational terms as a new miracle drug. . . . It is not surprising that many psychiatrists in private practice report a demand by patients and the public for this hallucinogen as a form of treatment. We question whether the serious dangers and unproven effectiveness of this drug have been sufficiently publicized. . . .

The medical and scientific literature indicate, and our consultants in psychopharmacology believe, that as yet there is no reliable proof that Lysergic Acid Diethylamide is a reliable adjunct in psychotherapy. . . .

We are of the opinion that the enthusiasm of some for the effectiveness of this drug is unwarranted at this time and should be questioned.

South of Rome the Emperor Hadrian constructed a vast labyrinth of rooms, gardens, fountains, and colonnades—the largest, most luxurious, and certainly the most peculiar memorial ever left behind by a single man

The Emperor's Monumental Folly

By MARY CABLE

"Under his reign, the Empire flourished in peace and prosperity," says Gibbon of the Emperor Hadrian. "He encouraged the arts, reformed the laws, asserted military discipline, and visited all his provinces in person. His vast and active genius was equally suited to the most enlarged views and the minute details of civil policy. But the ruling passions of his soul were curiosity and vanity."

Hadrian has been dead for more than eighteen hundred years, and nearly all the achievements of his "vast and active genius" are null and void and forgotten. But evidence of the passions which ruled that genius—boundless curiosity and unembarrassed vanity—still survives, particularly among the ruins of the most sumptuous, most extensive, least cozy, most odd and remarkable country seat ever built—Hadrian's Villa at Tivoli, outside Rome.

Not a great deal is known about Hadrian's personality—he wrote an autobiography but it is lost, and his only ancient biographers lived in the second and fourth centuries, some time after his death. His public and military accomplishments can be pieced together from contemporary letters, coins, and inscriptions, but to find out what he was like as a man is much more difficult. This amazing villa of his, which he built for his own personal delight and solace, is the closest thing we have to a memoir—even though in its very ruined state it makes enigmatic and abstract reading.

If you approach Hadrian's Villa along the route prescribed for tourists, you encounter, first of all, an enormous masonry wall (see page 36). Its dimensions are so imposing—about twenty-eight feet high and more than seven hundred feet long—as to raise your hopes that these ruins will not be very ruined. But after you have passed through a gate, you perceive that the wall is just standing there by itself, like an upsided ruler, and that on the other side of it is simply a very big, rectangular, grassy space containing a pond. There are various ruins in the distance, but here there is not a statue, not a column, not so much as a stone-on-stone. If you consult a guidebook, you find yourself called upon to imagine that this huge rectangle is enclosed by three more walls, that these walls, plus many marble columns, are the supports for splendidly painted porticoes, that the grassy space is enriched by flowers, statues, fountains, and that here and there the courtiers of Hadrian are strolling or marching about getting up an appetite for lunch.

This is only the beginning of a considerable job of imagining. Ahead, spread out on the rolling plain that skirts the Sabine hills, lie one hundred and fifty acres of thoroughly ruined ruins. Much more is still to be excavated, for it is known that when Hadrian died, in A.D. 138, his Villa covered more than seven square miles, three-fourths the area of Rome itself. This was not a villa in the modern sense, but a collection of building complexes: an out-of-the-ordinary sort of town, long on splendidly decorated piazzas, domed halls, and belvederes, and short on the more usual amenities, such as bedrooms, kitchens, and nurseries. The place has been called the Versailles of the Caesars, but Versailles, for all its glitter and show, was essentially a house; while the Villa seems an abstraction, an assemblage. Hadrian was, as Tertullian said of him, *"omnium curiositatum explorator";* as a student in Greece, a soldier in Dacia, a governor in Asia Minor, and a Roman emperor traveling in every corner of his empire, he was a tireless collector of beautiful things, and he needed a place to put all the treasures,

At the heart of Hadrian's Villa was a round pool with a central island, reached only by drawbridge, containing odd-shaped rooms. From this quiet retreat, historians surmise, the aging Emperor governed an empire then enjoying, thanks to his tireless energy and skill, its last great period of tranquillity and power.

THE BOY: AN ESSAYIST'S VERDICT

Hadrian had so many statues made of his favorite, a young man named Antinoüs, that they set an artistic style of male beauty for many years to come. A modern writer passes a harsh judgment on him, however, in her near-poetic essay on the Villa.

It is in the neighborhood of the libraries that you think of Antinoüs . . . the beautiful boy from Bithynia, Hadrian's love. . . . But what his statues announce and glorify is sex, and less a fulfillment than a long languorous exacerbation, a voluptuous delay such as Tivoli had never heard of before. A new kind of experience has come in: the romantic obsession, and wrapped in a sensuality the very opposite of Roman; this sultry shepherd child could only have come from the East. . . . It is a lush Middle Eastern handsomeness, even rather gross, and more than anything, empty; you could take him for a young Armenian rug salesman, or for King David, and this is curious because the shape of the face is new, and unique; you would know it anywhere. . . . The face, crowned with the richest ringlets yet seen in art, bends just a little downwards as in the resignation of the captive, nostalgic for a happiness he is no longer fit for and can scarcely remember. . . . The spring and tension of the perfect body have vanished; this one would change its pose only to sink, to fall, though in build it suggests great strength, more than any Apollo; it is broad-shouldered but passive . . . no little sleeping hermaphrodite, but a power to be shown on a scale with Hercules, a subtle and murderous triumph of the female principle. . . .

—*Eleanor Clark*, Rome and a Villa, *Doubleday 1950*

and copies of treasures, that he brought home with him. If he could have collected the Acropolis and the pyramids, one feels he would have done so. His particular passion was architecture. As an ordinary man putters in his tool shop, Hadrian, on the plains of Tibur, puttered with life-sized domes and vaults and peristyles, sometimes copying, more often improvising, but always building for building's sake and for the sake of housing statues and paintings.

Hadrian began traveling and sight-seeing at an early age. Born in A.D. 76 in a Roman province of Spain, where his family were Roman settlers, he went to Rome at the age of ten, on the death of his father, and was educated there under the supervision of his two guardians, one of whom was Trajan, at that time an important military commander. Hadrian's tutors were Greek, and they inspired him with a lifelong love for Greek culture; his schoolmates called him "the Greekling." When he grew up, Athens, not Rome, was his favorite city, and most of his Villa is of Greek derivation.

At fifteen Hadrian returned to Spain, and at nineteen began his long public career by serving as a tribune at the particular section of the Roman frontier that is now Budapest. Three years later, in A.D. 98, Trajan succeeded Nerva as emperor, and in A.D. 100 Hadrian was married to Sabina, Trajan's great-niece and nearest living relative. It was generally assumed that

Hadrian would succeed Trajan, but Trajan lived seventeen more years and not until he was on his deathbed did he make Hadrian his official adopted son and heir.

Hadrian himself had no son. His closest favorite was a young man named Antinoüs, and there are those who see in the Villa much evidence of Hadrian's devotion to him (statues of Antinoüs seem to have been there by the dozens). The childless and unhappily married Emperor, at any rate, put all his tremendous energies into work and continual activity. Until he was well into his fifties—an old man, by Roman standards—he went on traveling, often marching great distances and sleeping in the open. From Scotland to the Euphrates, from the Rhine to the deserts of North Africa, everywhere he went he collected—not only objects but ideas. And one can imagine that during this time he amused himself by planning the great Villa that was to be an end-of-the-road for all this traveling and collecting.

Such a forgathering of the world's most talented craftsmen and artists or such an amassment of precious materials has rarely been seen in the world before or since. Whole porphyry columns came by galley from Egypt, and from the quarries of North Africa, great slabs of serpentine, *giallo antico,* and alabaster. It was quite impossible for Hadrian to be too lavish with himself; the notion that an emperor could be criticized for not watching expenses had not yet occurred to anyone.

THE EMPEROR: A NOVELIST'S EVOCATION

The Emperor speaks in his own voice through the pages of an extraordinary novel, first published in French twelve years ago, which takes the form of a memoir—an attempt to re-create imaginatively the lost autobiography Hadrian actually wrote.

I have done much rebuilding. To reconstruct is to collaborate with time gone by, penetrating or modifying its spirit, and carrying it toward a longer future. . . . Our life is brief: we are always referring to centuries which precede or follow our own as if they were totally alien to us, but I have come close to them in my play with stone. These walls which I reinforce are still warm from the touch of vanished bodies; hands yet unborn will caress the shafts of these columns. The more I have meditated upon my death, and especially upon that of another [Antinoüs], the more I have tried to add to our lives these virtually indestructible extensions. . . . The Villa was the tomb of my travels, the last encampment of the nomad, the equivalent, though in marble, of the tents and pavilions of the princes of Asia. Almost everything that appeals to our taste has already been tried in the world of forms; I turned toward the realm of color: jasper as green as the depths of the sea, porphyry dense as flesh, basalt and somber obsidian. The crimson of the hangings was adorned with more and more intricate embroideries; the mosaics of the walls or pavements were never too golden, too white, or too dark. . . . Each structure was the chart of a dream. . . .

—*Marguerite Yourcenar*, Hadrian's Memoirs
Farrar, Straus and Co. 1951

Hadrian did not die at the Villa. Even in the last stages of illness he was restless, and death came to him while he was on a short trip to Baiae, on the Bay of Naples. But if he called any place home, it was surely this vast toy at Tibur. Perhaps it was too distinctively his ever to seem homelike to anyone else, for his successors do not seem to have spent much time there. The Goths, in the sixth century, used the Villa as a fortress. Subsequent barbaric devastations alternated with long periods when the Villa was a sleeping-beauty's castle, left to the vandalism of weeds and vines. People forgot what it was. The peasants of the neighborhood supposed that it had been a Roman town, and when they needed building stones or ornaments for the new, nearby town of Tivoli, they got them from there. In 1538 Cardinal Ippolito d'Este began to build the Villa d'Este at Tivoli. The architect, a Neapolitan named Ligorio, took much inspiration and a good deal of adornment from the ancient Villa for the new one.

As early as 1461, Pope Pius II, paying the ruins a visit, wrote that "the sublime and vast vaults" remained. "Time has marred everything," he went on. "The walls once covered with embroidered tapestries and hangings threaded with gold are now clothed with ivy. Briers and brambles have sprung up where purple-robed tribunes sat and queens' chambers are the lairs of serpents. So fleeting are mortal things!" It was not only time that marred things at Hadrian's Villa. Although the barbarians had taken away what was easily portable, such as candalabras, plates, and jewels, and the citizens of Tivoli had managed to move a few larger items, it was left to the popes, cardinals, and princes of the Baroque age to abscond with whole mosaics, inlaid marble floors, columns, capitals, and statues.

By the eighteenth century, when ruins and archaeology became a fashionable intellectual interest and English noblemen made the Villa a scheduled stop on the Grand Tour, nearly everything beautiful that had been in sight had been carted away. Piranesi's engravings show parts of the Villa looking just about as they do now, except much weedier. The stucco ceilings, like those at Pompeii, inspired the British architect Robert Adam, who went home to adorn the great houses of England with the delicate stuccowork of the Romans. Here and there at the Villa are bits and pieces of ceilings which seem so typically Adam and eighteenth-century that it gives one a shock to realize they are fifteen-hundred-odd years older.

During the eighteenth century two families who had farms in the area turned archaeology into a paying business. The Fede family, whose house was more or less on top of a Temple of Venus, sold what they excavated to wealthy Romans; for example, sixteen marble columns and a colossal Antinoüs now in the Vatican, and two marble gladiators that eventually found

A museum has been created for what is left of the Villa's statuary: left, a copy of an original Greek Hermes; right, a copy of a Greek Ares; background, a caryatid and a satyr as a young boy.

A visitor to the Villa comes first upon the single wall left standing (below) of the "Pecile," once a rectangular piazza with a pool in the center and a portico running all the way around.

their way into the hands of one of the Saxon kings of Poland. The Bulgarini family, owners of a large part of the ruins, sold excavation rights until legally restrained from doing so late in the nineteenth century. They kept businesslike records of everything that was looted, and these records have been a great help to modern archaeologists.

During this time of enthusiastic but unscientific investigation a lot of conclusions were jumped to, and various parts of the Villa were given identifications that, though wrong, have stuck. The official guidebook goes on using these labels, prefixing them with "so-called" and adding to the general confusion. Thus, the vast rectangle at the entrance gate is "the so-called Pecile." "Pecile" is a word derived from the Greek *stoa poikile*, or painted portico. It was thought that this area was a copy of the Stoa Poikile in Athens. Subsequently it has been pointed out that the Athenian painted portico was of quite a different shape and size and that Hadrian was not attempting to reproduce it, though he may have been inspired by it.

The so-called Pecile appears as flat ground, but under its southwest end is a three-storied honeycomb of small rooms, the "so-called Hundred Rooms" (actually there are a hundred and sixty). These were storerooms, servants' rooms, and guards' rooms, and were—and still are—connected with a network of underground passageways that traveled all over the Villa. The lower orders at the Villa were lower orders quite literally—living their lives in their dank dormitories or padding back and

forth through these service tunnels, emerging sometimes into the glitter and sunshine of some sumptuous apartment to deliver a cooling drink or wield a peacock fan.

These humid, dark "Hundred Rooms" are just the right sort of place for growing mushrooms, and a few years ago the then Supervisor of the Ruins, anxious to supplement his modest civil-service salary, started a private business of renting them out to mushroom growers. It was not until some archaeologists discovered the tenants were making structural changes in their mushroom cellars that the matter came to public attention and fungus growers and supervisor alike were removed from the premises. This same enterprising public servant allowed a camping site to be established directly next to the Villa, so the gentle country sounds that have always been there—songs of birds, goat bells, the braying of donkeys—are now supplemented and sometimes drowned out by the campers' radios.

In Hadrian's day the predominant sound was that of splashing water. No part of the Villa was without one or several fountains, and after the water had performed its assigned acrobatics, the Emperor's practical engineers caused it to flow through the latrines and thence away through sewers. One part of the Villa, shaped like a hippodrome and known since Cardinal d'Este's time as "the Stadium," was carefully excavated a few years ago and found to have been a garden, enhanced by many fountains and pools. At one end a tremendous fountain, something like the Fountain of Trevi, cascaded down a semicircular bank of steps that looks very much like seats in a stadium. The fountain basins bear traces of blue paint, which must have made the water as blue as a Hollywood pool.

Next door to this garden is an area known as the Fishpond Quadriportico. Here, a large pond—possibly it was a swimming pool—was enclosed by a quadriportico built on two levels. The upper level was a roofed colonnade and the lower, below ground level but lit by high-up windows, was a cool and airy tunnel for walking on hot days. This architectural caprice, known as a cryptoportico, was a favorite with Hadrian. Psychologists, attempting to analyze the Emperor across the centuries, have said that his love of shadowy places, of the interplay of light and shade, and of the inconstant constancy of running water, indicates a tendency to restlessness, ambivalence, even schizophrenia. They point out also that the Villa is schizophrenically planned: it has no harmony as a whole but is divided into aesthetically unrelated complexes. Each building is oriented to sun and view rather than to its neighbors.

If certain aspects of the Villa seem to indicate that Hadrian

The Villa sprawled over an area three-quarters the size of Rome. In trying to imagine its grandeur and extent, from the shabby ruins now standing, the modern eye is aided by a model located near the entrance (seen below, in part). Marked in white are locations shown in the photographs: (A) the wall of the Pecile (see opposite); (B) the "Island Nymphaeum" (see page 32), and (C) the Canopus valley with its pool (see pages 38–39).

was eccentric, others are monuments to his genius. For example, a certain room in the "Bath Complex" is regarded as one of the wonders of ancient architecture: its walls form an octagon, with alternately straight and convex sides, and its ceiling once soared dizzily for nine free-flying yards—a distance never achieved before and rarely since. Now, only a skeletal remnant of the vaults remains, and where the bathers used to congregate, great chunks of fallen masonry lie like burned-out meteorites.

One of the most splendid parts of the Villa, known as "Canopus," has been thoroughly excavated only in the past ten years (see pages 38–39). All evidence agrees that here Hadrian set out to represent Canopus, a sanctuary of the Egyptian god Serapis, which lay at the head of a canal on the Nile, near Alexandria. It was a place the Emperor must have remembered with particular fondness and poignancy, having visited it in the company of his beloved Antinoüs, who drowned shortly afterward.* Hadrian represented the canal by digging a basin, about 390 feet long, in the hollow of a small valley, and filling it with water. For many hundreds of years this basin was filled in and grown over, but the recent excavations have cleared it and brought up a fine haul of statues that once stood at the water's brink: four caryatids, copies of those on the Acropolis in Athens; two heroic-sized Sileni, with baskets on their heads; reclining figures representing the river Nile and the river Tiber; a life-sized crocodile, carved in cipollino, a marble whose green mottling makes it the ideal medium in which to sculpt crocodiles; copies of famous works by Phidias and Polyclitus; and much more.

The small valley that contains the water basin of Canopus rises steeply on two sides and at one end, and at this end Hadrian built an amazingly elaborate nymphaeum, or fountain building. What we see of it today is an enormous, ruined half-dome (hemicycle), beneath which a honeycomb of odd corridors and niches retreat into the hillside. In Hadrian's day an aqueduct brought water to a distribution tank at the highest point in this building, from whence it flowed through corridors, cascaded down walls, splashed into basins, spurted from niches, and ended by joining the large, placid pool of Canopus. At the lower reaches of this Niagara, sheltered by the outer rim of the half-dome, was an open-air dining room, a semicircle of stone couches where the Roman elite might recline and, while gorging themselves, admire the statues and columns reflected in the pool, the glittering domes of the Villa and, beyond, the same gentle hills and limpid sunset we see today. One wonders if

* It is not known whether Antinoüs died accidentally, was killed, or committed suicide. Opinion also differs as to his relationship with the Emperor, although most writers—among them both Eleanor Clark and Marguerite Yourcenar (see pages 34 and 35)—assume it to have been sexual.—Ed.

there wasn't a lot of random spray, but perhaps on a summer evening this would have felt refreshing.

Across yet unexcavated fields to the right and in back of the great nymphaeum are two more self-oriented parts of the Villa. The "so-called Tower of Roccabruna" is—or, rather, was —a three-storied square building with a ramp inside it and a belvedere at the top. Hadrian's purpose in building it, as well as the significance of the medieval name of Roccabruna, is lost in time. (One suspects that Hadrian simply wanted to see what a three-storied square building with a ramp inside it and a belvedere on the top would look like.)

On the highest point of ground in the entire Villa is the "so-called Academy"—*not* an academy, but modeled architecturally on the Academy at Athens. It was perhaps built for the Emperor to live in during very hot weather, when the sheltered slope below was not airy enough. One can imagine him being carried in a litter to this expensively adorned hilltop for a breath of humble fresh air. Some of the finest of the Villa's works of art were found at the "Academy," including the famous mosaic showing two doves on the rim of a vase, which since 1745 has been in the Capitoline Museum. The Academy complex includes, besides the usual waterworks and courtyards, a well-preserved theatre. No less than three theatres have been found at the Villa, but no stadium or arena, from which we may be safe in assuming that chariot races, gladiatorial fights, and the public disposal of Christians were not among the Em-

Partially restored, the southern end of the long pool called Canopus is ornamented with casts of statues found there. In building it the Emperor was apparently re-creating a shrine on the Nile, beloved to him for its associations with Antinoüs.

peror's preferred diversions. Not that he didn't believe in the extermination of Christians—at the celebrations marking the opening of the Villa, a Christian woman and her seven sons were put to death. But, on the whole, human-blood sports were not in Hadrian's line. One feels that they did not shock him, they merely bored him—although not as much as they bored his adoptive grandson, Marcus Aurelius, who used to take a book along whenever duty called him to the Colosseum.

The scale of these ruined courtyards and grand buildings suggests anything but a private place to live. In fact, there is only one corner of the entire Villa that looks as if it were built for privacy, and that is the extraordinary moated island that archaeologists are now calling the Island Nymphaeum (see page 32). In the lee of the slope where the grand peristyles overlook the Vale of Tempe, a twenty-foot circular wall encloses a circular colonnade; the colonnade borders a circular moat about ten feet wide, and in the middle of the moat is a circular island about eighty-two feet in diameter. The dates on the bricks, corresponding to A.D. 123, reveal that this was one of the first constructions at the Villa—perhaps it was something that the Emperor, who led a very public life, had especially longed for.

The moat was crossed by two drawbridges which, it is thought, were raised when the Emperor wanted to be alone, or perhaps when he and his intimates wanted to swim around the island. The bridges were certainly there for reasons of privacy rather than safety, for a child could have stormed this delicate marble fortress. What each small room was used for can only be conjectured: for sleeping, for reading, for making love, for commanding the Roman Empire. But certainly this was a *sanctum sanctorum,* and you feel, as you cross the stone bridge now there, that had you been alive in Hadrian's day, you would never have got near the place and even now are trespassing.

The moated island is sheltered from wintry winds by its great wall; and nearby is a small, sheltered bath that includes a heliocaminus, or room for sun-bathing. This circular room had five great windows in it, facing south, and the floor was heated. Marble seats, arranged in tiers as in a stadium, are still fairly intact, and if you sit here on a bright winter day, you can feel the sunshine gathering force, warming you just as it warmed the Emperor himself. Here, between timeless sun and timeless stone, the past seems to stir a little. Elsewhere in the Villa you have come much, much too late; but in sun's terms it is scarcely later at all. Hadrian was here just this morning.

Mary Cable, an American now living in Bangkok, has written for HORIZON *on several famous abodes—the Grand Seraglio, Blenheim Palace, and the castles of Ludwig II of Bavaria.*

Matzenauer as Brünnhilde, Braun as Wotan at the Metropolitan, circa 1890

The New Look

I began to understand the megalomaniac genius of Richard Wagner one hot, humid afternoon seven years ago in Bayreuth, when I first stepped into the ugly Festspielhaus, which has the worst seats and the best acoustics on earth. (The bad seats were designed by Wagner himself for the sake of the good acoustics.) I took in—it wouldn't be correct to say, "I heard," or "I saw," or "I felt," because it was a sensation for many senses, and for the intellect as well as the emotions—I took in the first scene of *Das Rheingold*, which had been a traumatic experience since my early operatic days, with unpleasant memories of corpulent Rhine Maidens chasing each other "through greenish twilight."

At the start of this production, staged by Wieland Wagner, one of the composer's two immensely gifted grandsons, there was darkness in the auditorium, which gradually filled, during the prelude, with the music of the waters of the Rhine. When the curtains parted, the stage seemed submerged under blue-green waves, ebbing and flowing in precise synchronization with the music. The Rhine Maidens were pretty and slim, wearing golden one-piece bathing suits, and as Woglinde sang "Weia! Waga!" I realized there were no props and stage sets—the whole scene was created by means of projected film and lights. This was truly Wagner's "total theatre"—the music, the singing, the water, the lights, and the sounds blended together. The instrumental groups of the orchestra seemed beautifully integrated, and the only, very minor flaw—a somewhat subdued sound of the first violins—was welcome proof that this was a real, human undertaking, and not something unreal, coldly perfect. Right then I felt that Wagner's grandsons had given his work a new lease on life.

No other artist has made such ferocious demands upon his performers and his public. Richard Wagner, an autocrat, not only wrote the libretto and the music (often with total disregard for the human voice) but also flung into the score his

in Valhalla

By JOSEPH WECHSBERG

detailed stage instructions,* which for a century remained the Holy Bible to Wagnerian producers. In 1895 Wagner's widow, Cosima, wrote to Houston Stewart Chamberlain, the well-known English protofascist, about an essay, *Concerning the Staging of the Ring*, by the noted stage designer Adolphe Appia: "The stage instructions are in the score and therefore Appia's work has no value for us."

In Richard Wagner's world everything takes on exaggerated proportions which ordinary human beings often have trouble understanding: the beauty and the boredom, the emotions and the pathos, the climaxes and the alliterations, the vocal and instrumental demands. The stage is populated by heroes and dwarfs, giants and gods, shining knights and evil monsters. And the music! Whereas Bach comforts you with his granite architecture, Mozart takes you to heaven, and Beethoven moves you with his tormented heart, Wagner overpowers you with the exuberance of his passions. Once he said that during a good *Tristan* performance the audience should go mad.

The physical demands alone are staggering. *Rheingold*, often given without intermission, lasts about 138 minutes; the first act of *Götterdämmerung*, 105 minutes; the first act of *Parsifal*, 102 minutes. In *Lohengrin* Ortrud is asked to stand in a prominent spot through a whole act and to sing only a few lines in an ensemble. Wagner has ruined more singers than any other composer, dead or alive. During my Vienna claque days we used a stop watch to time Wotan's

* Sample instruction, from the end of *Götterdämmerung*: "Brünnhilde has mounted her horse and leaps into the burning funeral pyre. Crackling flames go up, while the fire fills the space in front of the hall and seems to spread into it. Terrified, the men and women crowd together in the foreground. When the whole stage seems to be filled with fire, the red glow suddenly dies out and there remain only clouds of vapor which move toward the back of the stage and stay there as dark clouds. At the same time the Rhine rises over its banks, and now its floods submerge the scene of the conflagration. The Rhine Maidens appear on top of the waves. Hagen, who has watched Brünnhilde with mounting fear, becomes alarmed as he sees the Rhine Maidens. Hastily he throws away spear, shield, and helmet and jumps like a madman into the waters."

FESTSPIELE, BAYREUTH

A scene from Act III of Wieland Wagner's glowing 1962 version of Lohengrin

monologue in the second act of *Die Walküre*—about 20 minutes, and when badly done it sounded much longer.

Brünnhilde, the greatest woman Wagner created, makes her first entrance in *Walküre* with the taxing shouts, "Ho-yo-to-ho," topped by a ringing high C that would be difficult even after suitable acclimatization, and it's murder for any soprano who has stage fright in her throat. Unless the high C is there, pure and free and soaring, Brünnhilde is a flop no matter how hard she tries later on. And if Isolde sings her high C's in the first act ever so slightly off pitch, she is no longer a queen but just another *hochdramatische* soprano who isn't *hoch* enough. We have been lucky: we had Kirsten Flagstad and now we have Birgit Nilsson to give the perfect acoustical and visual illusion.

Wagner's heroes have similar problems. Siegfried must act and sing like a superman while he forges together the broken pieces of his sword, *Nothung*. Few men look attractive with a bearskin over their naked torsos and fewer still can sing the devilishly difficult "Schmiedelieder." Lauritz Melchior succeeded, and so does Wolfgang Windgassen. But when a *Heldentenor* fails, he looks foolish as "he cleaves the anvil from top to bottom with one blow" and the anvil doesn't come apart—or it does, three seconds *after* the stroke. Such accidents can happen in the world of Wagner, with its imperceptible line between the heroic and the idiotic.

The *Meister* had a magnificent sense of dramatics. He knew how difficult it is to get the people into the theatre and wanted to keep them there right to the bitter end, which is even more difficult. All his mature works, with the exception of *Parsifal* (a *Bühnenweihfestspiel*, or "stage consecration festival"), end with overpowering climaxes and the finest music. In *Rheingold* it is "Entry of the Gods into Valhalla." *Walküre* has a great love duet at the end of the first act; but you can't go home, for better things are still to come: "Wotan's Farewell" and the "Feuerzauber" ("Magic Fire" scene), which makes happy kids out of blasé operagoers.

In *Götterdämmerung* Wagner piled climax upon climax. After Siegfried's death and the thunderous "Funeral March," which always makes me look for the nearest exit, there comes the overpowering "Immolation" scene. After Brünnhilde has walked into her funeral pyre (a scene that has brought about the downfall of many a Wagnerian director), the whole music of the tetralogy is summed up in a glorious apotheosis, while the world of Wotan comes to an end in a cloud of atomic greenish-red, and then the waters of the Rhine fill the stage again, as in the very beginning of *Rheingold*—truly a grandiose conception. *Tristan und Isolde* ends with the "Liebestod," which is so good that it survives even concert performances. And in *Die Meistersinger* there is the great climax on the festival meadow.

And the same Wagner who gave us the witty and ironic libretto of *Meistersinger* (which shares these qualities with Da Ponte's libretto for *Le Nozze di Figaro*, Boïto's for *Falstaff*, and Hofmannsthal's for *Der Rosenkavalier*) also

Left to right: Materna, an 1887 Brünnhilde (horse unidentified); a band of

wrought the incredible beauty of *Parsifal* and so affected all music after him, from Bruckner and Mahler to Schoenberg and Berg, including those composers who tried hard to stay out of the charmed circle. Wagner had the artistic vision of the timeless genius. One no longer smiles to read that his early followers compared his *Gesamtkunstwerk* ("total theatre") to the work of Aeschylus and Sophocles.

He felt himself misunderstood (genius always does), and near the end of his life was so disgusted with the indifference of the German people toward his Hall of Fame in Bayreuth that he seriously contemplated emigration to America. But he also misunderstood himself when he prepared his immortalization while still alive. Long after his death the people who had been around him were so terrified of breaking tradition that they almost ruined Wagner.

My own problem with Wagner is that a considerable part of his work seems uninspired, pompous, monotonous and—let's face it—boring. I sit restlessly through Isolde's hate-love outbreaks in the first act of *Tristan*, and the hero's feverish hallucinations in the last act tire me to death. I don't enjoy the slow-motion gestures and endless monologues in the first act of *Walküre* while I wait for the love duet, and then I spend two unhappy hours waiting for "Wotan's Farewell" which, however, is worth all the waiting. As I get older, the waiting periods get longer. Fanatical Wagnerians (or Wagnerites) claim that not a single note must be cut in the *Meister*'s work. When Wieland Wagner, who knows more than any other man about his grandfather, years ago suggested that some of Wagner's earlier scores might be trimmed, there was a revolution in Germany and several *Generalmusikdirektoren* refused to conduct if a single bar was omitted. Wieland infuriated them by declaring, "If Richard Wagner were alive today, he would do a lot of cutting." During the first Bayreuth festival, in 1876, Richard Wagner actually told his artists, "Children, create something that is forever new. If you stick to the past, you will

Ring singers from Rheingold; *Hans Breuer as the hair-tearing dwarf, Mime*

PHOTOGRAPHS Opera News

be a sad bunch of artists." This was not always understood, even by artists. During the Nazi regime the composer Hans Pfitzner, who should have known better, called for a law "to protect works of art against willful desecration."

I have a hunch that my mixed emotions about the *Meister* are shared by many people who admire the beauty, passion, and sweep of his music but are repelled by what a disrespectful American friend of mine calls "Richard Wagner's Hippodrome—his imperious, stupendous, humorless demands for dragons, ships, swans, fire, suspended Rhine Maidens and collapsing castles, grandiose holocausts and clanking armor." I surmise my friend is secretly unhappy because he senses instinctively that he is missing something beautiful by his inability to get closer to Wagner.*

The late romantic designers never were able to get out from under the *Meister*'s spell; and—to quote my American friend again—they "produced those lugubrious horrors that delighted beer-filled Teutons of the period of Böcklin and made me cringe when, as an innocent boy in New York, I was given a ticket and subway money to take me to a sulphurous Saturday matinee of *Walküre* at the Met."

My friend should have been at the Vienna Court Opera in 1902 when the "Ride of the Valkyries" was performed by officers of the Imperial Guard, wearing false wigs, helmets, and armor. (The metamorphoses of the "Ride" in Vienna during the first half of this century are symptomatic of the problems of staging Wagner, whose specific stage instructions state, "A flash of lightning breaks through a passing cloud; a Valkyrie on horseback is visible in it; over her saddle hangs a slain warrior.") The Imperial Guardsmen rode across the stage on the Court's white Lipizzaner horses. The Opera's *Direktor*, Gustav Mahler, a fanatical perfectionist, ordered the horses brought to the opera house in the morning to get conditioned to stage thunder and lightning.

* The friend quoted is the editor of this magazine, and he is secretly happy about what he has missed.—Ed.

Shortly before the performance the horses were taken around the opera house so there would be no "incidents." Unfortunately, horses suffer from stage fright as much as people. The Lipizzaners behaved properly during rehearsals, but at night they were often unpredictable, with lamentable results.

After the era of the Lipizzaner-and-Imperial-Guard, Alfred Roller, Mahler's celebrated stage designer, took over. He constructed a sort of merry-go-round and placed chorus boys dressed up as Valkyries on wooden horses. While the stage hands turned the merry-go-round, there were awesome bolts of lightning and deafening crashes of thunder. The action took place behind a dark veil. Through openings in the veil the enchanted public could see the "Valkyries" galloping away. Viennese Wagnerians called it "the greatest ride outside of Bayreuth." There, under the severe stare of Frau Cosima, real horses were still used in obedience to the master's sacrosanct stage instructions. Ten years later Roller designed a new *Walküre* production, this time using papier-mâché figures of flying horses—early Mobiloil style—and sexy pin-up Valkyries. Their contours were dramatically silhouetted against a white backdrop and lighted by flashes. In Herbert von Karajan's current production of *Walküre*, for which Emil Praetorius designed the sets, the "Ride" is symbolized by lightning flashes and thunder and, above all, by Wagner's music, which conveys the illusion to today's audiences much better than any stage director could.

The Rhine Maidens in *Rheingold* have been another insoluble staging problem over the decades. In the early years of the century special flying machines were built for the three Rhine Maidens at the Vienna Opera. The machines, and the well-fed ladies who sang the parts of Woglinde, Wellgunde, and Flosshilde, were hung on steel cables from the rigging loft and swung about over the darkened stage. The cables had to be tested carefully before each performance, but Gustav Mahler was not happy because the singers became frightened and airsick, and often missed their cues. In a later production the singers were placed behind rocks, to be heard but not seen, while slim members of the *corps de ballet* were whirled through space. The dancers wore costumes decorated with phosphorescent paint and had orders to move their lips as though they were singing.

In the world's great opera houses Wagner is still staged in a backward way that exudes a museumlike flair—realistic and stylized elements mixed together, foolish sets, and ludicrous rock formations. In Vienna Karajan conducts the music of *Der Ring des Nibelungen* beautifully, but his failure as director proves again that Richard Wagner was right when he said that conducting and staging were arts that exclude each other. Music is basically an introverted art and staging an extroverted one. Richard Wagner could well have conducted the first *Ring* in Bayreuth, but he wisely limited himself to the staging and let Hans Richter conduct.

In Karajan's current *Rheingold* production, the old goldfish-bowl trick is performed again. The scene looks like a

George London (left) as Flying Dutchman, with Wieland Wagner

large aquarium with three lonely sardines swimming through the greenish waters, while Mesdames Lipp, Jurinac, and Rössl-Majdan stand backstage and sing "Weia! Waga!" Similarly this past season's production of *Meistersinger* at the Met showed the looming towers and pointed gables of Ye Olde Nuremberg, and my un-Wagnerian friend was worried about "the singing archers whose weapons constantly threatened to get into each other's eyes."

For half a century Richard Wagner's Hall of Fame carried on in the sacred tradition and almost became the mausoleum of Wagner's fame. In 1951 the grandsons, Wieland and Wolfgang, took over. They had the courage to admit that you cannot direct Richard Wagner in the 1950's as in the 1930's or the 1890's. Wieland's first productions of *Parsifal* and the *Ring* shattered all precedents. On the bare, *entrümpelt* (uncluttered) stage there were almost no props. The exception was the gold of the Rhine, which is a symbol, not a prop. There was a drake in the earlier years of the *Ring*, but he vanished between festivals.

Wieland created three-dimensional effects with lights. His heroes and Valkyries acted with sparse, stylized movements. He shocked German womanhood when he declared that the Rhine Maidens didn't have to be blond and Nordic but had to look well, act well, sing well. The Wagner brothers shaped a new type of Wagner singer who looks the part, has the needed vocal resources, knows the meaning of the words that go with the music, and expresses every nuance with the right volume of voice and a minimum of gesture. The singing actor (or acting singer) must also behave throughout the opera as a member of the ensemble. If such artists are not available at a certain time, the Wagners will postpone a production rather than use substitutes.

Wieland Wagner, who calls himself in the German equiva-

lent of *Who's Who* "painter, stage producer (autodidactical)," paints with light as other painters do with color. The "light organ" above the stage, forty projectors in the rear of the auditorium, and floodlights of extra-high intensity supply him with twenty-two colors and innumerable intermediate hues. Lights build whole rooms and create special moods. When the giants, Fafner and Fasolt, take away Wotan's daughter Freia, the goddess of youth, whom her loving father has traded in payment for his new castle, and the dusk of the approaching twilight of the gods covers the stage, the wizards of Bayreuth call up a somber mood by reflecting the stage lights on the cyclorama. Wieland uses light to give form and atmosphere to the music and the drama: certain lighting effects go with certain musical phrases (though the audience is never aware of the combination because it is so unobtrusively done). To Wieland the color of a costume is as important as the sound of a cello to the conductor, and a false shade as painful as a wrong note. His lighting scores are as complicated as the scores of the musicians. He uses darkness as a dramatic antidote to light, unlike many operatic directors who don't really know their business and, when in doubt, escape into merciful dimness or mystic ambiguity. Such ambiguity confuses the audience and has given the Germans a reputation for being deep when they are merely being vague.

In Bayreuth Wieland and Wolfgang are not merely not vague; they have creative ideas and they prepare thoroughly —five hundred solo rehearsals are held, thirty stage rehearsals with orchestra, seventy stage rehearsals with piano, and hundreds of chorus and lighting rehearsals for the five-week festival.

Opposition to the neo-Bayreuth productions now comes mostly from the conservative young groups in Germany who accuse the grandsons of betraying *Werktreue* (the faithful spirit of reproduction) and, oddly, also from young people who feel that the revolution has been "betrayed" and has become instead an evolution.

"If the young conservatives would read Richard Wagner's scores and writings carefully, they would discover that *Werktreue* was not in his vocabulary," Wieland says. "He knew that the theatre must be the true reflection of its time, free from all restrictions. We do not consider his stage instructions a sort of last will. They should help us to decode his scores and explain how he saw the perfect performance *in his day*."

Sometimes things go wrong in neo-Bayreuth, and when they do, they go wrong on a Wagnerian scale. The noted critic Willy Haas writes, "There is much *intra muros* criticism in Wieland Wagner's productions—the kind of criticism that one can level only at one's own grandfather, and which is basically nothing but a secret form of self-criticism. . . . To treat the genius as something vital and expose him to the transformation of the age: that is what I call the truly conscientious way of administering an inheritance."

It was the grandsons' good luck that they were born after the death of Richard Wagner and were never oppressed by a powerful grandfather image. As boys, they earned pocket money by secretly showing visitors the grave of Richard Wagner (he was just "Richard Wagner" to them, not Grandpa), and spent it for *Wurst* (sausage), a great treat since they were brought up as vegetarians. When their father, Siegfried Wagner, forbade them to look at *Tristan* ("that's not for children"), their interest was really stimulated. At the 1936 festival, when Wieland was nineteen and already had some revolutionary ideas of his own, he was shocked by the pseudo-naturalistic forests, the papier-mâché castles, and the fat ladies in their big helmets. "I drank in the music and closed my eyes so I wouldn't see the dreadful goings-on on the stage." Many people feel the same way.

"Some critics ask what Richard Wagner would say if he could see our productions," Wieland says. "What would Beethoven say if he heard Toscanini's performance of his Ninth Symphony? Because we use modern means to create dramatic illusion—choreography, geometric abstractions, typical colors, and symbolic forms—we are accused of being 'Americanized' or 'Bolshevized.' Such amusing words oversimplify the problems of interpreting Wagner today."

From the cleaning up of the props and papier-mâché castles it was a logical step to the removal of the romantic make-up. In its stripped-down décor, Richard Wagner's work becomes timeless (and timely) drama. In their searching analysis the grandsons want to prove that Richard Wagner's prophetic vision held up a mirror to the German people. Wotan, surrounded by Valhalla's walls and noble leitmotivs, emerges as a supergangster. According to Wieland: "He orders a castle he cannot afford, commits robbery to pay for his debt, cheats and lies, breaks promises to get the ring to gain power over the world, and banishes Brünnhilde, who might have saved him. Sounds familiar, doesn't it? And Siegfried, the ideal Aryan type, all muscles and no brains, runs out on Brünnhilde and is poisoned and brainwashed by the Gibichung crooks. During two acts of *Götterdämmerung* Siegfried is drugged—a handicap, at the least, for an intelligent actor-singer. Only shortly before his death does he become lucid again and briefly emerge as a great tragic figure."

Such heretical theories hardly endear Wieland to the proper Wagnerians in Germany, who hate the grandsons for shattering their romantic illusions. Yet the parallels are there. Wagner's Wotan appeared half a century before Hitler committed every possible crime "to gain the world." Hagen and his storm troopers were on Bayreuth's stage long before the days of Himmler and his S.S.

Wieland Wagner knows that most people attend Wagner performances for the romantic music and not for the intellectual truth, yet there is truth even in Richard Wagner's music. In Wieland Wagner's latest production of *Tristan und Isolde,* Isolde dies standing up, her arms crucified over Tristan's body. To his critics Wieland answered that Rich-

Simplified décor for the 1962 Bayreuth production of Tristan

ard Wagner never speaks of Isolde's *Liebestod* but of her *Verklärung* (transfiguration). In this, his sixth *Tristan* production, Wieland has come to the conclusion that the work's central theme is not the death wish but glorification of ecstasy. It's all in the score: Isolde's last words are not of death but *"höchste Lust"* ("the highest passion").

The musical truth is not in the leitmotivs that have become such a cult among Wagnerians, but in the musical keys. Each of his mature works is characterized by such a key: *Rheingold* by E flat major, *Walküre* by D minor, *Siegfried* by C major (also the key of Walther von Stolzing, the hero in *Meistersinger*), and so on. The E major key expresses erotic love; F major, love of one's country; and the demoniac D minor key (which Mozart uses to describe Don Giovanni's ruin) appears both in *Walküre* and *Tristan* when the hero is doomed. And between the *Lohengrin* Grail in A major and the *Parsifal* Grail in A flat major there is the progression of a lifetime of genius.

Wieland Wagner is now preparing his new *Ring* for 1965 and searching for new meanings. Furtwängler once admitted to Wieland that he had never arrived at a definitive reading of Wagner's late works, which offer constant challenge and a chance of evolution. Wieland sees his new *Ring* as "a series of visionary dreams.

"Instead of doing it with lights I want to use three-dimensional effects—modern paintings, plastics, and sculptures," he says. "I don't know what will emerge but it will be the reflection of my feelings at that time."

*Joseph Wechsberg, who wrote "The Music of Friends" (*HORIZON, *November, 1962), is very nearly the perfect Wagnerite, eagerly sitting in on productions of the* Meister *in many opera houses.*

On Stage: WOODY ALLEN

The world began bedeviling Woody Allen twenty-seven years ago when it gave him Flatbush for a birthplace. In the years since, the universe has marshaled all the resources of the technological revolution against Allen and pommeled him into a five-and-a-half-foot, 125-pound, harassed, timid victim who has simply to step onto a night-club stage to make an audience weep with laughter. "I keep having this birthday-cake fantasy, where they wheel out a big cake with a girl in it, and she pops out and hurts me and gets back in." The comedian shifts his weight, blinks his eyes in the bright stage lighting, and lets a trembling hand adjust the thick spectacles and drift over the receding hairline. He stands unhappily with his hands in the pockets of his tweed coat.

"Two weeks ago I sold the memoirs of my love life to Parker Brothers, and they're going to make it into a game." Allen clutches at the microphone—holding it at arm's length to keep it from jumping at him—and resumes in his raspy, shaking voice, "I can take care of myself. In case of danger I have this cutlass that I carry around with me—and, in case of a real emergency, I press the handle and it turns into a cane so I can get sympathy." As the audience warms up, Woody Allen begins to look like a bantamweight fighter, the cracks rolling out tremulously, but with trip-hammer precision. "I was thrown out of the Boy Scouts myself. I tried to rub one stick together to make a fire. This is very Zen—but not Boy Scout. . . ."

Woody Allen is a man beset by the world; looked down on by portraits in the Metropolitan Museum; pushed around by waiters, women, hoodlums, cops, and electrical appliances—a Chaplinesque character who "went to Vic Tanny's for six weeks and nothing happened. So I figured why not give Tanny the cash and let him walk me home nights?"

Allen, who comes from a totally nontheatrical family—his father is a waiter and his mother a bookkeeper—sat down one day during his high-school years in Brooklyn to give some serious thought to his future—and started writing jokes. He sent the jokes to newspaper columnists; and a public relations firm, impressed with what they read in the columns, hired Allen to write gags at the rate of fifty a day for personalities who could not create their own witty responses to newspaper reporters. At age seventeen, still a high-school student, Allen was writing material for the radio and television shows of Peter Lind Hayes and Herb Shriner.

The following year he ventured into Manhattan and ended an exceptionally poor academic career by being ejected from New York University. He promptly began turning out material for Sid Caesar, Art Carney, Garry Moore, Buddy Hackett, Kaye Ballard, and Carol Channing.

Last year Allen was persuaded to perform his own material. He began his stage career at New York's Duplex, went on to the Blue Angel. the Bon Soir, the Crystal Palace in St. Louis, The Bitter End and the Village Gate in Greenwich Village. He has appeared on the Jack Paar Show, PM East, Open End, and the Tonight Show, and his performances are rapidly becoming as stylish as his writing.

Though Allen keeps a refreshing distance from politics, from Kennedy quips, from barbs about missiles and Berlin, he is a topical comedian. His topicality is sociological—set in the valley of tears that is populated with automatic elevators and electric toothbrushes—and his idiom is a peculiarly modern one: his irreverent gags unravel with the free-association spontaneity of a jazz musician. He states his theme, the modern man victimized, and launches into bizarre, razzle-dazzle variations in a rhythm that mixes "bop" with "New Orleans."

His subject and target are himself, and his comedy is that of the compulsive bungler, at odds with all the forces of the modern world. "I'm afraid of the dark. I can't fix anything. I have four lawsuits pending. I have overdue books at the library." Without flinching or smiling, with neither the hope of ultimate victory nor the sweet agony of defeat occurring to him, Allen sums up, "Once I tried to tip a process server."

Woody Allen now lives on New York's upper East Side, talking over coffee about process servers and his malevolent electrical appliances with the same disarmingly self-abnegating, slightly mad delivery he uses on stage. His style has been compared to S. J. Perelman, Robert Benchley, James Thurber, Mort Sahl, and Wally Cox; and none of the comparisons is helpful. Sahl and Allen have the same sort of nervous rapid-fire style, but Sahl, with his confident quips, is decidedly different from Allen, the worried, underweight boxer who always fights in the preliminaries, never the main event. And no comedian has ever been so consistently the hopeless butt of all the modern world's practical jokes. Chaplin could shrug it off. Benchley could enjoy his own joke. Thurber turned a neat phrase, and a trick, at the last moment. Wally Cox was able to surrender.

But there is no way out for the character Woody Allen presents to us. He is the pathetic little creature who gets up from the barroom floor again and again and again; he will never stay down, he will never conquer, and he will never give up. He is neither a winner nor a loser. He may, perhaps, teach us how to survive. Or, as Allen concludes his routine, "The message is God is love, and you should lay off fatty foods."   CHARLES L. MEE, JR.

On Stage: CARMEN DE LAVALLADE

The dancer Carmen de Lavallade has been referred to by an impressionable and somewhat unlimber critic as an endless curve. She is not, but a casual observer could be excused if he mistook her for one. Another canard frequently circulated about Miss de Lavallade is that she is beautiful. She is not beautiful either. She is handsome, arresting, exotic, and almost impossible to forget. But not conventionally beautiful.

She has something far more important than conventional beauty, however, and that is the ability to project her personality—or personalities. Miss de Lavallade has a way of living in other skins than her own, and she seems no less tangible in a Biblical drama, say, than as the splay-hipped strumpet she portrayed with such exuberance in the "Porgy and Bess" sequence from television's *The Gershwin Years*. In fact, the reason so many people are convinced that Miss de Lavallade is the things she is not, is that she has an uncanny ability to melt into a myth, leaving scarcely a trace of herself behind. She can *think* herself beautiful when she wants to—or think herself arrogant or snobbish or old or ailing. There is a remarkable close-up of her in the televised version of John Butler's *Portrait of Billie*, in which she interprets in dance the career of the late singer Billie Holiday. For one long moment the camera fastens on her face as it goes through a metamorphosis from tigerish fury to defiance to a kind of bewilderment to the slack dullness of despair. It is as convincing—and powerfully moving—an image as is likely to emerge from a television screen.

Not surprisingly, Miss de Lavallade is not an admirer of purely abstract dance. She believes that the dance should tell a story, and she has naturally gravitated to roles that are strongly dramatic. These have included an assortment of temptresses—which explains in part how Miss de Lavallade, who is shy, soft-spoken, and even somewhat withdrawn, has achieved a reputation for being a pretty incendiary number. The impression is perhaps enhanced by her style. She is tall, lithe, and graceful, and she moves with a fluent ease that many a dancer would like to emulate. It is essentially a lyric style, one that avoids the angular movement or the sharply staccato phrase. When Miss de Lavallade uncoils her long legato dance phrases, a critic could indeed imagine that he was watching an endless curve.

At an early point in her career Miss de Lavallade was employed by Ciro's night club in Hollywood, where she was called upon to do a rumba while smoking a cigar. That indignity notwithstanding, her rise to dancing eminence was remarkably swift. Although she was brought up in Los Angeles, where her father was a bricklayer, Miss de Lavallade counts herself "French, African, and a little German," a mixture that may account for the exotic flavor of a face often mistaken for West Indian. Her sister was a dancer, and so was her cousin, Janet Collins, and Miss de Lavallade got herself launched at the Lester Horton school of the dance. She appeared as a dancer in several films, the most illustrious of which was probably *Carmen Jones* and the least illustrious a vehicle called *Demetrius and the Gladiator*. But she was making little more than rent money before she auditioned for the Broadway musical *House of Flowers* in 1954. She was twenty-three.

House of Flowers provided her not only with her first starring role but with a husband. Geoffrey Holder, who was also in the show, married her, he has testified, because "I thought she was a snob, and I liked that; I like to go after them; I don't like them to go after me." Miss de Lavallade married Holder, she has testified, because he was "the most talented, temperamental man I ever knew." The marriage has resulted in a six-year-old son who has been dancing almost from the time he could toddle.

Miss de Lavallade has had all the work she can handle since *House of Flowers* closed. Her range has been wide: she has appeared, for instance, as soloist with the Metropolitan Opera Ballet, with Pearl Bailey in Las Vegas, in a pastiche called "Island Idyll" at the Radio City Music Hall, in the German composer Carl Orff's cantata *Carmina Burana* at the New York City Center, and with Alvin Ailey and his company in a program of ethnic dances that successfully toured Southeast Asia. She has also been turning her attention to television, and one measure of how important a commodity she has become is that CBS-TV bought out one night's performance of *Ballet Ballads*, in which she was starred, and closed the theatre in order to fly her to Key West, Florida, to film the "Porgy" dance sequence for *The Gershwin Years*.

Miss de Lavallade thinks of herself as a new breed in the theatre. She is not a ballet dancer, although she studies the classical ballet, and she is not really a modern dancer, although she studies with Martha Graham. She prefers freelancing to appearing steadily with any single company. Nor is she exclusively a dancer: she also sings, and has appeared in a straight dramatic role opposite Harry Belafonte in *Odds Against Tomorrow*. Unlike those unhappy creatures who feel "if they have to dance *Swan Lake* one more time, they'll throw themselves out the window," Miss de Lavallade believes that a girl has to be versatile to survive. And she is determined to survive. RICHARD W. MURPHY

Baron Haussmann did what no conqueror of the City of Light has dared to do—he virtually razed it.

Then he rebuilt it as the perfect setting for his master's glittering, though raffish, Second Empire

THE MAN WHO "DESTROYED" PARIS

On June 30, 1853, at ten o'clock in the morning, Baron Georges Eugène Haussmann put on his full-dress uniform—white trousers, dark blue coat, plumed hat, sword, silver braid and oak leaves—and drove to Saint-Cloud to be sworn in as Préfet de la Seine, the chief administrator of Paris. He had been appointed to realize Napoleon III's dream of transforming Paris from a medieval slum into "the capital of capitals."

"I could not hide my keen satisfaction," noted Persigny, the Minister of the Interior, about Haussmann's appointment. "Where the most intelligent, clever, upright and noble men would inevitably fail, this vigorous athlete, broad-shouldered, bull-necked, full of audacity and cunning, capable of pitting expedient against expedient, setting trap for trap, would certainly succeed. I rejoiced in advance at the idea of throwing this tall tigerish animal among the pack of foxes and wolves combining to fight the generous aspirations of the Empire."

Persigny's estimate proved correct. Haussmann's Paris was, in the end, Louis Napoleon's only lasting accomplishment. It miraculously survived Bismarck, Wilhelm II, and even Hitler, and it may yet survive the automobile. The foxes and wolves, however, are still influential. Even today, Haussmann is more often blamed than praised for building the magnificent city we know and love.

The *Guide Michelin*, for instance, has not one good word for him. It blames the prefect for "sadly spoiling" the Ile de la Cité and fusses about the missing elms in the Jardin de l'Elysée. The English critic John Russell, who has poured his delight for historic Paris into a charming book simply called *Paris*, pronounces Haussmann "one of the most obnoxious of recorded beings." The Baron, he writes, "butchered" the city: "the more recent ruins of Dresden and Rotterdam are hardly more sinister than those which we glimpse in photographs of Paris in the 1860's."

In his own time, the Emperor's political opponents inspired the charge that Haussmann was little more than an imperialist vandal who tore up romantic old Paris to build "parade streets" designed as shooting galleries in which to mow down unruly workers.

Reading the expressions of everyone present, one might be justified in thinking that Napoleon III had just signed a declaration of war, or perhaps made them all dukes. But no—he is merely handing to Baron Haussmann, the embroidered gentleman seen in profile, the decree for the annexation of the suburban communes in 1860. Despite the pomposity of Adolphe Yvon's painting, the moment was worth recording—for it gave Paris the boundaries and shape it has retained to this day.

By WOLF VON ECKARDT

This thesis still pervades most books on city planning. Lewis Mumford, in particular, has often complained about the allegedly mechanical pomposity of Haussmann's work. Only Robert Moses, the Haussmann of New York, has steadfastly rallied to the defense of the Baron—largely, no doubt, because the two are so remarkably similar in character, method of action, and their concept of what their cities needed at the time. Haussmann, Moses has written, "grasped the problem of step-by-step large-scale city modernization. He knew the close relationship between wide thoroughfares and bridges, slum clearance, water sewers and incidental utilities and public improvements, that . . . made Paris accessible and livable."

The method employed is now called "urban renewal." Both men commanded armies of demolition crews to attack the social and sanitary blight of slums, remaking whole sections of their cities to suit the needs and tastes of their time. Jane Jacobs, a brilliant and angry New Yorker, is in the vanguard of the current rebellion against urban renewal, which is now going on in just about every American city. In her book *The Death and Life of Great American Cities* she opposes all large-scale plastic surgery on the city organism, in part because of the temporary pain it causes but mostly because it destroys the character, variety, and liveliness of the old tissue. She would rehabilitate the old, rather than create a new urban design. The drab monotony of most of today's tall housing slabs, rising gauntly out of desert-like open spaces and devoid of the cozy bustle of the old street life, has given much validity to her rebellion. But one can also argue that both Haussmann's Paris and, to a lesser extent, Moses's New York stand as proof that drastic rebuilding is often not only necessary but also an expression of each generation's urge to make its mark on history.

Certainly, no rehabilitation of either the Paris slums or of New York's Lower East Side was feasible. Their cataclysmic destruction and replacement with new housing were vital to both cities. So were Haussmann's boulevards and Moses's parkways, the Bois de Boulogne and Jones Beach, the Paris Opéra and New York's Coliseum, even the Paris Exhibitions of 1855 and 1867 and the New York World's Fairs of 1939 and—hopefully—1964. The analogy has its limits, of course. All-powerful as he seemed in the days after the Depression, Robert Moses never had the power of the Prefect of the Seine. Nor could he operate on Haussmann's scale, much as he might have liked to. But while the work of neither produced great architecture, each in his own way answered the social and technical needs of his time. Each sought to make his city more efficient and livable. To achieve bold changes in any city pattern takes ruthless and cunning manipulation to override vested interest, lethargy, and conservative sentimentality. "One of the virtues of being known as an s.o.b.," Moses has said, "is that people leave you alone." Haussmann might well have said the same. He understood that it pays to cut corners and red tape with audacity. For to remake an obsolete city into a viable work of art is an audacious undertaking.

At the time Haussmann took over in 1853, nearly a million

By the mid-nineteenth century much of the Ile de la Cité had arrived at the parlous state above (the Rue de la Colombe, as photographed about 1850). Haussmann swept across it like a bulldozer, even though that useful word had not yet been invented, and left in his wake a set of gigantic administrative buildings—drab, intimidating, and dull, but undeniably more sanitary.

*Few stones were left unturned on the
Ile de la Cité, including those of the ven-
erable Hôtel-Dieu (below)—the oldest
hospital in Paris and possibly in Europe.
In typical fashion Haussmann razed a
wide area to the north (bottom), rebuilt
the hospital there, and then knocked
the old one down—dealing a blow to history
but improving the view of Notre-Dame.*

Parisians were crowded into an almost impenetrable labyrinth of decaying tenements and narrow, muddy alleys within the old walls at which the *octroi*, or duty on all goods entering the city, was collected. On the Ile de la Cité, according to the novelist Eugène Sue, the mud-colored houses were "broken by a few worm-eaten window frames which almost touched at the eaves, so narrow were the streets. Black, filthy alleys led to steps even blacker and more filthy and so steep that one could climb them only with the help of a rope attached to the damp wall by iron brackets."

By the time the new prefect was forced to resign in 1870, seventeen years later, he had drained the foul juices of these slums with his sewers. He had provided the city with fresh water. He had created beautiful new parks and green spaces. Most important of all, he had pierced the *octroi* wall, and the rotting jumble it confined, with a web of new avenues and boulevards which opened up the city to its growing suburbs, to light, to air, and to a rare order and design that make Paris seem a familiar place within hours after you first arrive. Nor need you fear great changes to come. For Haussmann's brilliantly conceived and ruthlessly executed thoroughfares have given his city a permanent structure which serves as a grand backdrop not only to its many magnificent historic buildings but also to the assertion of true city life—outdoor cafés, kiosks,

street vendors, and the whole gay bustle which we all enjoy but which our silly zoning restrictions and puritanical anti-city attitudes will not allow here at home.

Haussmann's arrival on the Parisian scene coincided with the emergence of the nineteenth-century social conscience. Karl Marx had just left the city for London. Pasteur was bent over his microscopes. Victor Duruy called for new schools "for our future industrial population." Courbet demanded a new realism in art, as did Pierre-Joseph Proudhon and Flaubert. And Baudelaire sought a new kind of beauty by wallowing in the very depths of the slums Haussmann was about to destroy.

There were still islands of seventeenth-century splendor, of course: the Place des Vosges, for example, and the Tuileries, and the Place de la Concorde with its fountains and flower beds. Here moved the Paris of high society and ostentation, the Paris of the Duc de Morny who, as president of the Corps Législatif, dominated the political councils as well as the salons, bedrooms, race tracks, and the stock exchange, and who was the arbiter of male fashion: he wore black waistcoats bound with gold.

Morny owed his influence to the circumstance of being the half brother of the new Emperor (even though Queen Hortense had never acknowledged this love child of her indiscretion with an illegitimate son of Talleyrand). And he owed his fortune to a liaison with the rich and beautiful wife of the Belgian ambassador, the Countess Le Hon. The ladies, following the lead of the Empress Eugénie, wore crinolines which often used such great quantities of costly material that, as the papal nuncio once remarked, there seemed none left for the bodice. And they drenched themselves with perfume, for their nostrils were understandably offended by the stench of the streets. The droppings of thirty-seven thousand horses, as well as human excrement, were collected in open cesspools and carted nightly and noisily across the cobblestones in leaking wagons to canal boats which transported the malodorous mess to the Forest of Bondy, six miles east of the city.

After the boredom of the Bourgeois Monarchy and the disillusionment of the Second Republic, Paris—all of France, in fact—was suddenly filled with nostalgic remembrance of Bonaparte's glory. Napoleon I had built the Bourse, the Madeleine, and a handful of other fine buildings, but he did not have the time to rebuild Paris itself, as Voltaire had demanded many decades before him. His Arc de Triomphe, at the end of the gloomy and unpaved Champs-Elysées and, at the time, of Paris as well, was still hung with scaffolding. Louis Napoleon owed his great popularity to the general feeling that he might restore some imperial glamour to both France and its capital.

The Emperor's new prefect was neither a professional planner nor an architect, but an administrator pure and simple (he held most of his expert advisers in these fields, which he grasped so well, in often justified contempt). Nor was Haussmann a real baron. His claim to the title required a stretch of the imagination which reached back to a maternal grandfather. But that was his only corruption. His vast public works programs were

When the far-spreading network of new streets and boulevards that Haussmann built (in red) is superimposed on a map of the city as it was, one can see how radical was his transformation of Paris. The map itself (schematic, and therefore not wholly accurate in scale) was published in 1847, six years before Haussmann went to work. Paris—the shaded area—was entirely confined by the octroi wall, where a tax was collected on all goods entering the city. Outside lay the independent communes of Montmartre, Grenelle, and so on, and beyond them the fortifications built in 1841–45 by the nervous July Monarchy. In 1860 Haussmann destroyed the octroi wall and merged the narrow roadways on either side to create the outer ring of boulevards. At the same time, the neighboring communes were absorbed and the city limits were pushed out to the fortified wall, where they still are (the wall itself was finally demolished at the end of World War I). Haussmann also gave Paris its parks (in green): the Bois de Boulogne (left), the Parc Monceau, the Parc des Buttes-Chaumont (upper right), and the Bois de Vincennes.

The drawing at left shows the
façade of a typical Paris apartment
house erected under Haussmann's
aegis, while the cartoon below shows
what went on behind it. On
the street level are the concierge's
quarters and shops. After that,
to ascend the stairs is to descend
the economic scale: the rich are
ensconced on the premier étage, the
merely prosperous above them,
the poor in smaller quarters on the
top floor, and the destitute up
in the attic along with the artists.

The Builder, LONDON 1858

56

Haussmann's activities naturally provided the cartoonists with a fruitful subject. Here are three satirical comments by the great Honoré Daumier. The one at the top refers to the hazards of walking in the streets. The middle one suggests that uprooted tenants had to take to the trees. The bottom one shows the effects of a visit to the Exposition of 1855. The couple in ballooning crinoline and frock coat is just going in, while the deflated pair at the right is just coming out.

as beset as any today by greedy real-estate speculators and building contractors, and they involved complex financial schemes. Yet his only personal gain after seventeen years in office was a modest pension and a chest full of medals he had received from visiting dignitaries.

He was born in 1809 into a fairly well-to-do and well-connected Protestant family originally from Alsace. His school, the famous Lycée Henri IV, provided him with the right education and the right friends. The poet Alfred de Musset was among his classmates. But although Haussmann boasted of this acquaintance and all his life wrote poetry (which those who read it found atrocious), he admits somewhere in the three dull volumes of his memoirs that no one can rightly claim he deserted the Muses in order to take up law and a civil-service career. He joined the Corps des Préfets (which Napoleon I established to extend centralized rule into the provinces) and became a fiend for road improvements and other useful public works. Before long, he acquired a mousy wife, to whom neither he nor anyone else seems to have paid much attention, and a reputation as a highly efficient and ambitious administrator, of which his superiors in Paris were well aware.

Haussmann was forty-two when the then Prince-President Louis Napoleon rewarded him with the highest position he dared hope for at the time—the Prefecture of the Gironde, which includes Bordeaux. He hastened to Paris to thank the President, who was even more enigmatic than usual. "I cannot at this moment tell you why I am sending you to Bordeaux," he said, his pale blue eyes inscrutable in his pasty face. "I want you to start tomorrow morning as early as possible. Fetch your instructions from the Minister of the Interior." That same evening, November 30, 1851, Louis Napoleon unrolled his papers marked "Rubicon," on which he had plotted the course to his late uncle's imperial throne. When Haussmann called at the Ministry the next morning, he found troops outside and, inside, not the old Minister, M. Thorigny, but the Duc de Morny, busy staging his half brother's *coup d'état*. Morny explained to his first caller that he was to secure Bordeaux for the President-turned-dictator.

The new prefect obliged, with his customary dispatch and with a minimum of arrests. When the Prince-President visited Bordeaux ten months later, he was greeted with discreetly planted shouts of *"Vive l' Empéreur!"* And it was in Bordeaux that he announced his program: *"L'Empire, c'est la Paix!"*

The idea of rebuilding Paris had probably first occurred to Louis Napoleon fifteen years earlier during his brief exile in New York. The July Monarchy of Louis-Philippe had unceremoniously dispatched him there after his first attempt to seize power in France by a military coup had failed. By chance he met a young man in New York whose identity, unfortunately, has slipped into the crevices of history. This young man showed him plans for a new city he wanted to build, "not house by house, as in Europe," but all at once. What these plans were like we do not know. Louis Napoleon, once his thoughts were directed toward such a project, may have remembered Rome, which he visited in his youth, as it had been rebuilt by Pope Sixtus V late in the sixteenth century. We know that he was greatly impressed by London. He lived there for two years between his escape from imprisonment in the fortress of Ham (the result of a second unsuccessful *Putsch*) and his final return to France in 1848 as a candidate for President of the Second Republic. He admired the new London—the rows of new monumental buildings in white Portland stone with their porticoes and sculptured fronts along the Strand, Piccadilly, and Regent Street, and the typical London squares which he later copied in Paris. He took home with him not only "Miss Howard," the pretty shoemaker's daughter from Brighton, but also some definite notions about city planning. He himself with "his own august hand," as Haussmann put it, plotted his ideas for Paris on a map in blue, red, yellow, and green crayons, denoting his order of priority. Those sketched in green were never executed. He kept a copy of this plan in each of his residences, but only one has survived. It was found in Berlin not long ago. The Emperor had proudly presented it to the king of Prussia during his visit to the Paris Exhibition in 1867.

Napoleon's plan shows a web of straight, wide roads criss-crossing the maze of the inner city in all directions. It is so remarkably similar to a present-day map of Paris that its boldness is at first not apparent. Yet it envisioned far more rebuilding than even the energetic Haussmann could accomplish in seventeen years.

The Emperor's concepts should not be ascribed merely to his fear of internal revolt or to a vainglorious edifice complex, although they include elements of both. The audacious Napoleon I, who feared nothing else, had feared a hungry Paris; since his downfall there had been eight occasions when barricades were thrown up in the streets of Paris, and three of them were followed by revolution. His far less audacious nephew frankly avowed that many of his avenues were based on strategic considerations. He and Haussmann cut them through some of the most restless workers' districts, made them wide enough for a troop of cavalry to maneuver in, and placed barracks for soldiers at key points, particularly near the Hôtel de Ville and on the Place de la République. It would seem, however, that the two men often claimed defense against angry mobs to induce parliament and the city council to vote the appropriations for their expensive enterprises. At any rate, whatever military security they sought eluded them; the Empire was toppled by Prussian soldiers, not by Parisian workers. Napoleon III has been called, correctly, "the Well-Intentioned" and "Saint-Simon on Horseback." He knew that his best defense was economic prosperity and that this, in turn, was largely achieved by public works that provided not only his empire's sumptuous stage sets but also public health, housing, and employment.

If he accomplished little in Paris before Haussmann arrived on the scene, it was not for lack of trying. Within weeks after his *coup d'état* in 1851 the city council approved his plan to enlarge the Louvre, to build the hundred-foot-wide Boulevard

TEXT CONTINUED ON PAGE 63

BOULEVARDS AND BOULEVARDIERS: THE WORLD OF HAUSSMANN'S PATRON

The empire of Napoleon III, unlike his uncle's, was subjected to the cold scrutiny of the camera as well as to the flattering regard of the official artist, and it is in old photographs that it comes most vividly to life. Its early days are perfectly evoked by the picture opposite of three dandies entering the Rue de Castiglione (built by the first Napoleon and architecturally superior to any of his nephew's streets). More typical of its later years is the panorama overleaf, showing Haussmann's broad new Avenue de l'Impératrice (now the Avenue Foch) filled with an afternoon throng of strollers and carriages streaming out to the Bois de Boulogne. The Second Empire had a somewhat specious glitter; its tone was no doubt ostentatious, bourgeois, even a little arriviste. *But for all that, it was a more genuinely brilliant period than anything known to the Republics that have succeeded it.*

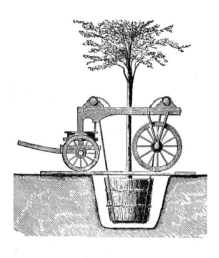

*The calculated pomp of the Second
Empire often had to find a vehicle in
social events, since Napoleon III
had fewer victories to celebrate than
Napoleon I. One of the rare occasions for bugles and drums, seen opposite
from a roof top, was the return of
the troops from the Italian Campaign
of 1859. This small war was the
Emperor's contribution to the unifi-
cation of Italy; he came to the
assistance of the Sardinians, and together they defeated the Austrians
at Magenta on June 4, 1859. Sardinia
acquired Lombardy, Napoleon III was
rewarded with Nice and Savoy, and the
name of the battle was bestowed on
a strident purplish-red shade of dye
that was invented the same year.
Another invention, but one related to
Haussmann's campaigns instead of
Napoleon III's, is the tree-planting
machine above. It could handle
a thirty-foot tree in full leaf, and a
battery of them turned raw new
streets into shady avenues overnight.*

TEXT CONTINUED FROM PAGE 58

de Strasbourg, and to erect a Palace of Industry. Less than a
year later work on the Bois de Boulogne was under way. But
the actual execution of these plans was largely frustrated by
a prefect and city council who resented the expense. In their
first talk, following the ceremony at Saint-Cloud, the Emperor
urged Haussmann to dissolve the council and appoint a planning commission. Haussmann refused; he would not rouse the
foxes and wolves before he had properly entrenched himself at
the Hôtel de Ville. The Emperor was not angry. As always, he
listened and, undoubtedly, admired his new prefect for the
qualities he himself lacked—strength and decisiveness.

A curious friendship developed between the two. The prefect
always had direct access and was in as close contact with the
Emperor as any of the ministers. He used such rare tact and
fervent enthusiasm in telling the Emperor just exactly how to
realize his dream of the "capital of capitals" that in the end
it was difficult to say just whose dream it was. He creatively
refined Napoleon's concepts, which were only colored lines on
a map, to advance his own sound ideas of city planning in all
its social as well as aesthetic aspects.

His first year in office was a year of preparation. Then
"Haussmannomania," as the journalist Jules Ferry called it,
broke out. In the summer of 1854 Paris began to shake with
the noise and fury of excavations, demolitions, grading, construction, political fights, expropriations, and speculation.
Haussmann's procedure was much like that used by urban
renewal authorities in this country today: a municipal surveyor
would appraise condemned properties and fix the compensation
to be paid their owners. Once the matter was settled, the city
sold the land to builders who were under contract to demolish
the old buildings and erect new ones that conformed to Haussmann's specifications. His regulations mostly concerned appearance—building lines, street elevations, and building height; he
paid little attention to what happened behind the façade, where
all too often builders put crowded and airless tenements. But
the regulations did include certain standards of maintenance.

This transformation was divided into three stages, or *réseaux*,
as Haussmann called them. The first, a number of projects
within the old city, was authorized before 1858 and financed
with state aid. The second, the so-called 180 Million Agree-
ment, provided the great traffic arteries for which the state paid
only a third. The last was a sort of mopping-up operation which
Haussmann paid for with his complex and controversial deficit
financing, borrowing against the estimated future growth of
the city. Altogether he spent two and a half billion francs, or
what would be just under two billion dollars today.

This huge expenditure was a matter of deliberate government
pump priming. France had just come out of a depression and
a revolution; the Emperor and his Saint-Simonian advisers
were set on a period of peace and public spending to assure
speedy recovery and to ward off another depression. Since the
conservative banks, notably Rothschild's, were reluctant to
supply the necessary capital, Napoleon III created his own
source for investments, the Crédit Mobilier. This institution

*Next to the imperial couple
themselves, the two most glittering
figures in the raffish social world
of the Second Empire were the Duc de
Morny (top) and the Countess
Castiglione (above and opposite). Morny
was an illegitimate half brother
of the Emperor, and noted for his good
looks, manners, waistcoats, race
horses, and addiction to women—not
to mention a very slight talent
for writing operettas. Countess Castiglione played peekaboo with a
great many men, but only if it seemed
likely to get her somewhere. It
got her to the top: she was for several
years the mistress of Napoleon III.*

floated multimillion-franc bond issues to finance his plans for Paris. Haussmann's predecessor, Berger, was shocked at the then novel idea of "productive spending" by which the city would borrow money, "invest" it in public works, and then pay off the debt with the rising tax revenues that the growing population and the increased property values were to create. Haussmann, though, had no qualms about this arrangement and, in fact, soon claimed it as his own idea.

In the first few years, however, he still played it safe. He financed his first *réseau* by floating another loan, drawing on a surplus in the city budget, and encouraging private investors. The second *réseau* was in part financed by state funds but, in the face of rising costs and Haussmann's growing appetite for more and more projects, expenditures soon outgrew appropriations. The legislature was reluctant to vote more money. So the Emperor in 1858 authorized a new organization called the Public Works Fund which could float bonds in its own name; such restrictions as were imposed upon it were always waived because Haussmann had a way of introducing the matter at the very end of the legislative session when the weary delegates were ready to pass anything.

But even this fund was not sufficient to finance the prefect's plans. He therefore evolved increasingly complex and daring methods of contracting with private construction companies and enabling them to raise capital on municipal credit before a project was even started. As a result, Haussmann was able to contract a half-billion francs' worth of projects without legislative authorization.

In the end the Senate reproached him for these manipulations. Haussmann confessed only to the sin of being "too much carried away by the passion for unprecedented results which would be one of the glories of a great reign." These results included some thirty miles of avenues and boulevards, the completion of the Louvre, new market halls, and a new opera house. There was the Bois de Boulogne, the Parc Monceau, the Parc des Buttes-Chaumont, the Bois de Vincennes, and the fresh water and sewage disposal systems which became the envy of the world.

Haussmann's new arterial streets made it possible to cross Paris quickly all the way from Neuilly in the west to Vincennes in the east, via the Champs-Elysées, the newly widened Rue de Rivoli, the Rue St. Antoine, and the Place de la Bastille. The north-south arm plowed through the decayed heart of the city, creating the Boulevard de Sébastopol, crossing the Ile de la Cité as the Boulevard du Palais, and cutting through the Latin Quarter as the Boulevard Saint-Michel. The intersection of the two great thoroughfares was near the Hôtel de Ville, where Haussmann created generous open space that still accommodates the heavy traffic quite nicely.

This project cleared the Ile de la Cité, which had been an incredibly congested slum and, at the time, a hangout for criminals (see pages 52–53). Not that everyone admires the results. In building the Boulevard Saint-Michel, which cut through the then equally slummy Quartier Latin, Mumford

charges that Haussmann, "in the interest of mechanical efficiency and outward esthetic conformity . . . took the simplest of all methods of improving one portion of it: he wiped it out."

A good many of the other new boulevards and avenues radiate from the Etoile, where Haussmann created not only an essential and generous traffic circle but also—as you had better not try to confirm while driving in that mad whirl—a most imposing setting for the Arc de Triomphe. To achieve symmetry and a coherent design, he created seven additional avenues and imposed strict architectural discipline on the surrounding houses. Designed by the architect Jacques-Ignace Hittorff, they are no masterpieces—and Haussmann knew it when he hid them behind two rows of trees. But the virtues of uniform height and conforming façades became obvious when higher buildings were later permitted in the second row on the Champs-Elysées side; they are like blotches on a Piranesi etching. Haussmann was particularly proud of the Etoile and recommended that it be viewed from atop the Arc.

From there you can also see the two most prominent of his many other streets: the Boulevard Malesherbes, which joined the new suburbs with the city; and the Boulevard Haussmann, which (with the Avenue de Friedland) runs from the Etoile to beyond the Opéra, an area he developed intensively. The Boulevard Haussmann, where the Galeries Lafayette, Au Printemps, and other department stores and a number of big (but no longer fashionable) hotels are now located, was the last of the projects to be completed. The final three hundred yards were not laid until 1924.

But most of the work proceeded with astounding speed. Long sections of the boulevards were complete with mature trees within a few years. These trees seem to have caused the only serious difference of opinion between Napoleon III and his prefect. The Emperor disliked trees (just why is not chronicled), but Haussmann fortunately favored them enough to have a special, most ingenious tree-lifting machine invented which could transplant trees thirty feet high (see page 63). He devoted special attention to selecting the right species, and they are today among the splendors of Paris.

To architectural finesse, on the other hand, he paid little attention. His interest, unlike that of most American architects today, was in the appearance of the *street*, the elegance of the total urban design, rather than in the originality of the individual building. He did not employ any outstanding architects, largely because there were none better than the likes of Hittorff, a Rhinelander with a thick accent, for whom he had little respect. Yet, in the end, Hittorff quite handsomely provided what Haussmann wanted: inconspicuous but nicely patterned façades with even skylines crowned by modest mansards. The apartments behind these façades were, of course, often poorly lighted and awkwardly laid out by our standards. But so was most housing of the period, and many people still prefer these now ramshackle but spacious apartments with their twelve-foot ceilings to glass-walled efficiencies.

Nor are the Haussmann boulevards and avenues as monoto-

In the flamboyant Opéra, the Second Empire left its perfect monument. Haussmann's demolitions to clear a place for it began in 1860 (above), but the building itself did not get under way until 1861, and for the next eight years it rose slowly behind scaffolding (opposite). When the Empire collapsed in 1870, the Opéra was still no more than a shell; it was completed by the Third Republic in 1874. The cross section below shows the complexity and size of this theatre, which for sheer grandiosity is still unmatched.

nous as his critics charge; they were designed for a variety of different uses which give them life at all hours. The top floors of most of their buildings provide what today we would call "low-income housing"; then come "middle-income" accommodations; and on the street level there are stores. Our own type of zoning, in contrast, lets most streets be used for one purpose only. We segregate commercial activities from our residences, and our residences by income groups. People don't mix. Everybody on the street does the same thing at the same time. Even such an exciting street as New York's Fifth Avenue becomes a dark desert after the stores have closed. But Parisians love the unexpected, and don't mind living below less privileged people and above a café.

Haussmann was particularly concerned about perspective and lines of vision. He had the church of Saint-Augustin built just to provide a focal point for the broad Boulevard Malesherbes. And he was most annoyed that the dome of the Sorbonne chapel barely missed being in the line of sight of his Boulevard de Sébastopol. American planners often forget that, aside from aesthetics, such points of orientation and identification help people find their way around in a city and give it its distinct character and "image."

The Louvre had been under alteration ever since its beginnings as a fortress in the twelfth century.* Napoleon Bonaparte saved the palace from Republican destruction and cleared away the slums that shouldered the Tuileries. His nephew proudly completed the complex by joining the Tuileries (later burned down by the Commune in 1871) to the old Louvre. It

* See "The Louvre" by Allan Temko, in HORIZON for September, 1960.

COLLECTION GEORGES SIROT

Le Monde Illustré, PARIS 1875

was difficult, because the new wing along the Rue de Rivoli was not on a parallel axis with the old one along the Seine. The architect, Louis Visconti, solved the problem by designing two hollow blocks which are parallel on the court side but do not have identical plans: the outer wing of the northern block follows the angle of the Rue de Rivoli. When Visconti died, his successor, Hector Lefuel, saw fit to enrich the design with a façade more ostentatiously sculptural than any of the older ones. It became the *dernier cri* in architecture. Spread by the Ecole des Beaux-Arts, Lefuel's neo-baroque Second Empire style was imitated in luxury hotels and millionaires' villas all over the world—except, oddly enough, in Paris itself. Only one contemporary critic, the Swiss art historian Doctor Wilhelm Lübke, spoiled the fun. The new French style, he remarked, "tends toward ever greater decadence . . . the hectic desire for novelty drives Frenchmen to all kinds of experiments which, because the political life is held in rigid chains, try to make up in other areas of cultural activity."

The architectural influence of Les Halles, the central market, may not immediately have been any greater, but it has subsequently proved to be far more significant. This was among the first large iron-and-glass structures in history. Just before Haussmann was appointed, a city architect, Victor Baltard, had designed for the market an utterly impractical Roman stone fortress with massive masonry walls and slit windows. It was the laughing stock of Paris and the Emperor pulled it down. He personally suggested a modern building similar to Paxton's Crystal Palace in London, which had given glass and iron their first practical trial. Baltard balked. How could he compromise himself, he asked, with building materials that neither Brunelleschi nor Michelangelo had used? But Haussmann thundered: *"Du fer, du fer, rien que du fer!"* And, surprisingly, the same Baltard came through with a design that used the structural potentials of iron and glass not only quite honestly but without even trying to look "classic." When the Emperor expressed his pleased surprise, Haussmann replied: "The architect is the same, but the prefect is different!"

The buildings are still standing, though not for long. By the end of 1965 the picturesque market will be moved to different sites outside the city, and tourists will have to finish off their nights on the town with onion soup somewhere else.

Haussmann was criticized at every step. The newspapers and opposition speeches charged excessive spending, exorbitant contractor profits, cruel dislocation of people, unfair assessments, rising wages, and skyrocketing rents. Property owners often complained bitterly, of course. But once their property was condemned, they could win nothing but higher compensation. Haussmann used resolute skill in dealing with (and at times circumventing) the city council and parliament, which held the purse strings. The prefect resisted the pressure for rent control (which he called a "socialist idea") and for direct building by the government (he needed the investments of private contractors), and was able to prove that he built far more houses than he tore down. Despite his statistics, however, the housing

Napoleon III's Paris is seen at its most graceful in the water colors of Constantin Guys, who painted the Three Women in a Calèche *below. "One knows of Parisiennes," wrote a contemporary, "who would certainly die every evening if they did not go for a ride every afternoon around the lake. It was not for them a habit but a need. From two to four in winter and from five to seven in summer . . . the beautiful ladies circle the little lake like squirrels in a cage, but more slowly; they look at each other, bow to each other, and tear each other to bits."*

shortage remained acute—in part because the building boom attracted more and more out-of-town workers, in part because, just as today, cheap tenements were all too often replaced by expensive luxury apartments. Nor did wages ever quite catch up with the rising cost of living. But Paris was never gayer.

Parvenus and the true aristocracy alike amused themselves with charades and table tipping, but probably enjoyed their clubs and salons more. The Jockey Club, to which the elegant Morny belonged, was the most fashionable. Its greatest cultural achievement was that it was responsible for Richard Wagner's most celebrated failure in Paris. Its playboy members patronized opera, but tardily and chiefly for the ballet, which they insisted should appear in the second act. Wagner was equally adamant about putting his *Tannhäuser* ballet in the first. He was all but run out of town for this impudence.

Among the other Jockey Club diversions were the "Ogresses," about a hundred of the Second Empire's most dazzling *poules de luxe.* They lived in shameless luxury, even appeared at court, and at times, as in the case of Marguerite Bellanger, found favor in the eyes of the Emperor himself. The line between *demi-monde* and the *haut monde* was frivolously blurred. It became a fad for great ladies to play the courtesan—and some didn't stop at playing.

The most scandalous of these ladies was the Countess Casti-

The cancan might hold sway on the stage and in the popular dance halls, but at the great balls organized by the municipal council of Paris in the Hôtel de Ville, one waltzed to the more decorous strains of Offenbach. The ladies were in extreme décolletage, the gentlemen were mostly in gold-frogged uniforms, and it all looks very elegant in this water color by Louis Eugène Lami— although these occasions have also been described, less sympathetically, as "a curious mixture of dynastic luxury, Caesarian ostentation, and the jumped-up middle classes."

69

glione (see pages 64, 65). She was very young and very bored, particularly with her husband, when Cavour sent her from Turin to Paris to see what she could do to encourage Napoleon III's sympathies toward the cause of Italian unity. Her first appearance at a reception in the Tuileries produced a sensation, repeated many times over on later occasions as the Countess progressively revealed her charms by lowering her décolletage and raising her hem. As Horace de Viel-Castel observed, "She carried her beauty with insolence and displayed her charms with effrontery." She won the Emperor—but not necessarily for Cavour's policies.

The official tastemakers were Princess Mathilde Bonaparte, the Emperor's cousin, and her unpleasant lover, the Count de Nieuwerkerke, a sculptor who became director of the Louvre. Mathilde's chief *raison d'être* was her salon, where she entertained the Dumas, *père* and *fils*, Sainte-Beuve, Flaubert, Viollet-le-Duc, the Goncourt brothers, Ingres, George Sand and, later, Maupassant and Anatole France. But of the real artistic life of Paris she knew little. It flowered beneath this upper crust. Daumier drew his acid caricatures. Courbet quarreled with the salon, and the Emperor did him the honor of striking his *Bathers* with his riding crop at a private showing because the central nude seemed to him too fat. Napoleon thought Manet's *Le Déjeuner sur l'herbe* immodest but bought a lyrical landscape by Corot. Millet was officially considered a radical. With Monet and Degas, he and many others ended in the Salon des Refusés, which opened in 1863 when Emile Zola's agitation and the fact that Nieuwerkerke had rejected more than four thousand paintings caused an open scandal. Only Jacques Offenbach—"a knife-blade with a large nose which was always crowned by glasses and a ribbon," as one writer described him —was equally acclaimed by all. Wagner said that Offenbach's music "released the odor of manure from where all the pigs of Europe had come to wallow." But the dislike was mutual and Parisians didn't care. His operettas were light, spicy fun and didn't require the effort that Wagner, Saint-Saëns, and Berlioz demanded of their listeners.

And everyone danced the cancan. "The music struck up, and then—I placed my hands before my face for very shame," wrote Mark Twain when he first encountered it in Paris a few years later. "But I looked through my fingers. . . . A handsome girl in the set before me tripped forward lightly to meet the opposite gentleman—tripped back again, grasped her dresses vigorously on both sides with her hands, raised them pretty high, danced an extraordinary jig that had more activity and exposure about it than any jig I ever saw before, and then, drawing her clothes still higher, she advanced gaily to the center and launched a vicious kick full at her vis-à-vis that must infallibly have removed his nose if he had been seven feet high. It was a mercy he was only six."

The International Exposition of 1855 epitomized it all and, in the bargain, established a new industry for Paris—tourism. For the first time signs proclaiming "English Spoken" appeared in the shop windows. At the helm of the invasion was Queen

In August of 1855 Parisians lined the Boulevard des Italiens (above) to watch a dazzling quartet roll by: Queen Victoria, Prince Albert, Napoleon III, and the Empress Eugénie. By returning a state visit from the imperial couple, Victoria became the first reigning British sovereign to visit Paris since Henry VI —and that was in 1431. Across the street is the famous Café Tortoni, the most fashionable—and agreeable— rendezvous for statesmen and men of letters from the beginning of the nineteenth century until it disappeared about 1887. Shown in a water color of the café terrace (right) are two habitués, the Duc de Morny and Prince Metternich (foreground).

Victoria who, with her self-defeating habit of underscoring for emphasis, wrote to the king of Belgium: "I am *delighted, enchanted, amused* and *interested,* and I think I never saw anything more *beautiful* and gay than Paris—or more splendid than all the palaces." Among the most splendid was the Hôtel de Ville, where Haussmann had his offices. For the ball in the Queen's honor he turned it into a lavish fairyland with carloads of flowers, miles of crimson drapery, and tons of candles. Nowhere else in the world was there such extravagant municipal hospitality.

Orsini's attempt on the life of the Emperor in 1858, near the old opera, called attention to its obsolescence and its dismal neighborhood. Haussmann, however, was given no money for yet another project. He proceeded anyway. He built the Rue Halévy from the Boulevard des Capucines, site of the Café de la Paix, to nowhere in particular. With the rues Scribe, Gluck, and Auber, it just happened to enclose the site Haussmann had in mind for a new opera building. Then he built a suitable approach—the future Avenue de l'Opéra—and successfully forced the issue.

The competition for the new building was held in 1860, giving the 171 entrants exactly a month to prepare their plans. Charles Garnier, who had worked with Viollet-le-Duc and who later also designed the Casino at Monte Carlo, was the winner. His excessively ornate, though well-structured, building is Second Empire at its most extreme. Although the imperial couple never entered it, as it was not completed until 1874, one would have expected the lush exterior alone to delight the Empress Eugénie. Not so. She was furious that her friend Viollet-le-Duc had failed to win the commission. Sarcastically she asked Garnier what style the Opéra was—Louis XIV, Louis XV, or Louis XVI? His answer was prompt: *"C'est du Napoléon III."* To the charge of excessive ornamentation he replied: "If I ever build a penitentiary, I assure you I will produce a façade so mournful that it will be less sad to be behind it than in front of it."

The new building, as *Le Temps* commented, shifted the real center of Paris in perhaps a symbolic way. "Originally it was around the cathedral," the newspaper stated. "With the monarchy it gravitated to the Louvre: with the Revolution to the Hôtel de Ville. Must we admit that the center of this powerful city . . . is today an opera house? . . . Are we no longer anything more than the capital of elegance and pleasure?"

Work on the Bois de Boulogne, which had been an "arid promenade" on the outskirts of town, had already started before Haussmann took office. It was the Emperor's idea, inspired by London. He wanted to surpass Hyde Park and did—again, thanks to Haussmann. The new prefect soon discovered that his predecessor had started excavations for the lake, on which Napoleon had set his heart, in such a way that it would drain away downhill. Haussmann's second discovery was a brilliant young landscape architect on his staff, Adolphe Alphand. His Bois remains a masterpiece of landscaping with its winding paths, streams, waterfalls, flower beds, pavilions, and cafés—

*The Universal Exposition of 1867
was Haussmann's last great triumph.
It was opened by the Emperor and
the Empress (above) and was visited
by a parade of crowned heads from
all across Europe—the rulers of Belgium, Prussia, Italy, and Russia—
and the Prince of Wales. After that,
Haussmann and the Emperor entered
upon their time of troubles; by 1870
one was fired, the other in exile.*

not to speak of the Longchamps race track—and is still the delight of many thousands. Haussmann soon balanced the feat at the other end of Paris, closer to its poorer inhabitants, with the Bois de Vincennes and the lovely Parc des Buttes-Chaumont which, before Alphand went to work, was a deposit of dung and filth. (The Regional Survey of New York in 1928 recommended one acre of park for every 300 to 500 inhabitants as a reasonable standard. Manhattan has one acre for every 1,500. Paris, in 1870, had one for every 390.)

Even royalty visited Haussmann's famous sewers, as tourists still do. Although the Emperor was totally uninterested, one of Haussmann's *petites amies* from the ballet was obviously infected by his obsession with this enormous project. She willed 400,000 francs for the construction of sewers in her native village. (A little old lady in Greenwich, Connecticut, once willed Robert Moses ten thousand dollars because his parkways gave her so much pleasure.) When Haussmann started, ninety-six drains (but not nearly enough) fouled the waters of the Seine. When he was through—as the result, he claimed, of a sudden inspiration during a sleepless night—every Paris street had its own covered drain. There were some three hundred miles of them, all well-lighted, clean galleries which now contain the water mains and telephone and telegraph cables as well. "The sewers of Paris are so fine," mocked Veuillot, "that something really great should happen in them."

Haussmann was equally successful with his battle for clean spring water. But it was a hard struggle. The Emperor, the people, and the legislature could not comprehend why the Seine was not fit for drinking. Only after a formidable job of persuasion and cajoling did Haussmann get his appropriation for eighteen and a half million francs to bring the waters from the Dhuys River across an eighty-one mile aqueduct. At lunch at Fontainebleau one day, he was teased that he, too, like so many others, should have been made a Duke. "I should be made Aqueduc," he replied.

Only one major project failed. The cemeteries of Montparnasse and Montmartre had become as overcrowded as the inner city was when Haussmann began. Nauseating smells pervaded the air, and the dead were at times exhumed after only five years. The prefect presented his plan for two new cemeteries outside the city which would allow room for expansion. The railroad, he proposed, could transport both the dead and their mourners. But by this time Haussmann's political powers began to fail him. His project did not survive the furor of polemics and protests it aroused. "A few years more and you will see a worthy completion of the system with the invention of steam engines for burying people," snorted a journalist. "The expropriation of the living is followed up by the expropriation of the dead."

The Universal Exhibition of 1867 was the apogee for both Haussmann and the Empire. "There was music in the air, life and action all about us, and a conflagration of gaslight everywhere," wrote Mark Twain. The people gaped at a roster of celebrities: the Prince of Wales, the King and Queen of Bel-

Haussmann's earlier Exposition of 1855 inspired the catalogue of marvels below—all very mid-nineteenth century. Whether one actually saw Swiss maidens, Turks, Arabs, Mandarins, Greeks, and Persians strolling about in these costumes is a moot point, but one can hardly question the huge jardinieres, the "lion et serpent en bronze," the bird cage, the parlor pipe organ. At the lower right is a guard, who appears to be armed with a feather duster—and with all that gimcrackery about, why not?

gium, Czar Alexander of Russia, the King of Prussia, and—"you could go nowhere without running into his enormous bulk," wrote Canrobert—Otto von Bismarck.

Haussmann received decorations from them all. He had headed the organization committee, and Alphand landscaped the exhibit site on the Champs-de-Mars. It was ablaze in chocolate and gold and displayed the new marvels of the dawning industrial age, although the greatest marvel of all was the new Paris.

Other French cities copied its boulevards, perspectives, and parks. Haussmann's influence was felt in Rome, Stockholm, Barcelona, Madrid and, across the Atlantic, in Mexico City. In this country it had a marked effect on the planning ideas of Daniel Burnham, Charles McKim, Frederick Law Olmsted, and the "City Beautiful" movement.

Encouraged by Louis Napoleon, Haussmann proceeded with more foresight and a better understanding of the nature of the city than any other planner who worked on a similar scale. He even advocated that a green belt surround Paris on which no

PROMENADE A L'EXPOSITION UNIVERSELLE DE PARIS. 1855.

sprawling urban developments were to be permitted. The idea
has been adopted by succeeding generations of planners the
world over. But it remains a dream and urban sprawl continues
unchecked. His pioneering in urban renewal was not only in
the realm of technical achievements—sewer, water, and traffic
engineering. He also understood, better than most of our urban
renewers today, that people expect monumentality and inspiration, as well as efficiency, of a city. He obtained legislative
authority to control the appearance of buildings and their relationship to each other in order to assure unity and order. The
individual buildings are not inspired, but together they form
a civic architecture that is. This concept seems still lacking in
American city planning today, which is concerned almost exclusively with the urban floor plan and hardly at all with the
elevation. Perhaps Haussmann's urban design is indeed too
straight, too mechanical, too uniform. But it is *design* on a
grand scale, and it proceeds from deliberate artistic intent.
Moreover, time's patina has mellowed it.

It mellows the critics as well. Even Lewis Mumford has come
around. "Think of the boulevards of Paris," he recently told
a meeting of architects, "those magnificent pieces of planning
that Haussmann carried through with such consummate skill
and such beauty. In my old age I have become a judicious
admirer of Haussmann, and I frankly avow that."

But Haussmann's enemies in the press and the Senate saw
only his consummate skill at manipulating the budget. The
Empire was in trouble and the prefect of Paris became the
scapegoat. "Haussmann lacks all sense of legality . . . he
breaks the law with abandon, you might say with coquetry."
And when he answered the attacks, the Republican deputy Jules
Ferry complained: "M. le Préfet does not argue with the newspapers, he drowns them . . . he crushes his enemies under the
weight of his milliards; he buries them under formidable statistics of pavements and macadam; he drowns them in a prodigious network of sewers and water pipes."

The election of May, 1869, gave the liberals a vast majority,
and Napoleon III was no longer in the mood to back his controversial protégé. He was dismissed to live out his remaining
twenty-one years as a moderately successful businessman.

But Haussmann was not about to leave his office without
ceremony. The opportunity came when the new Minister of the
Interior wished to meet the staff of the Hôtel de Ville. Haussmann's successor had not yet arrived, so the dismissed prefect
led his flock to the Ministry. "I set out in full uniform," he
recorded in his memoirs, "at the head of my cortège of gilded
carriages." To the stunned Minister he delivered an eloquent
speech. His employees, he wrote, were quite overcome and pro-
tested "their affection for me, whom, they said, they looked
upon as the real head, the honor, and the glory of the French
administration."

A student of the graphic arts and architecture, Wolf Von Eck-
ardt has written for HORIZON *on such wide-ranging subjects*
as calligraphy, the Bauhaus, and contemporary stained glass.

*Haussmann's Paris remains, although the
Second Empire and its way of life have long
vanished. Only on occasion do we get a
whiff of them, as of an old fragrance, from
paintings like Edouard Manet's* La Musique
aux Tuileries. *Who goes now to the Tuileries
Gardens to listen to music? But in 1862
apparently everyone did, for Manet included
not only himself (extreme left margin),
but the painter Henri Fantin-Latour (full-face
beside the tree), the poets Charles Baudelaire and Théophile Gautier (in front of the tree),
his brother Eugène (right of center, in light
trousers), who married Berthe Morisot, and (behind him) the composer Jacques Offenbach.*

NATIONAL GALLERY, LONDON

Great Confrontations ❧ II: Leo the Great and Attila the Hun

The majestic fresco painted by Raphael in the Vatican's Stanza of Heliodorus and completed by his pupils places the meeting of Leo and Rome. Intimidated by the calm presence of Leo (left) and by the apostles Peter and Paul hovering above him, Attila (right center) swivels

By C. V. WEDGWOOD

WHEN FORCE MET FAITH

In the second of the great rooms at the Vatican that he designed for Pope Julius II, Raphael painted the meeting between Pope Leo the Great and Attila, king of the Huns. The heathen war lord rides on a black horse at the head of his army. His trumpeters blow a fanfare. Behind him a burning village flames against a hillside. Over his head a red banner streams in the wind. Toward him comes Leo the Great. The Pope is mounted on a white palfrey and advances at a stately pace, escorted by two cardinals in flowing robes. One of his retinue holds aloft the cross. The saint emanates a monumental calm as he lifts his right hand in a gesture at once of defense and of blessing. The force which had destroyed Rome confronts the faith which would renew it.

The faith is justified. Attila reels backward in his saddle and the reins drop from his hands. His eyes are fixed on the threatening figures of Saint Peter and Saint Paul, who hover like avenging angels, with drawn swords, in the luminous evening sky.

The meeting of Pope Leo I and Attila took place in the year 452. Raphael painted the fresco between 1512 and 1514—more than a thousand years later. The event had by then long been enshrined in tradition as one of the great deliverances of Christendom. The heathen King of the Huns had been halted in his victorious march to Rome by the mere word of the saintly Pope. Legend had added a miracle to the bare outline of the facts. Attila was said to have seen Saint Peter standing behind the Pope, threatening him with a drawn sword. Raphael went beyond the legend and introduced Saint Paul, as well, into his picture—the two greatest Apostles descending from Heaven to guard the Eternal City.

The far-off event that Raphael chose to illustrate so magnificently cannot have looked like this in reality. Pope Leo had no cardinals with him. He went out to meet Attila as one of a deputation of three—the other two being secular dignitaries of the Roman state. The meeting did not take place, as Raphael depicts it, just outside Rome, but in northern Italy, not far from the modern town of Peschiera. No contemporary witness records either of the two heavenly apparitions. No contemporary witness records very much about the meeting at all, except that it took place, and that immediately after it Attila withdrew from Italy.

Later, tradition gradually invested it with symbolic meaning. The most ferocious of the barbarian invaders, the terrible Attila, had fallen back at the bidding of the Holy Father. Thus, in the hour of earthly defeat, when her material might was laid in the dust, the spiritual power of Rome shone forth and gained a bloodless victory.

This was the way in which, under the influence of ecclesiastical chroniclers, the event came to be seen. Skeptics may argue that the known facts hardly justify this interpretation. It is easy enough to show that the spiritual authority of Rome gave little protection against the barbarian invaders. Forty years before Attila raided Italy, Rome had already been taken and sacked by Alaric the Goth. Three years after the retreat of Attila, it was once more taken and sacked by Gaiseric, king of the Vandals.

Attila directly outside the walls of his horse and signals his warriors back.

But material disaster is not the whole story, and there is a kind of truth in the medieval tradition. In the collapse and destruction of the Roman world the Church provided what strength and what defense there was. Time and again, as the civil authorities failed and the imperial troops withdrew, Christian bishops came forward to reorganize the shattered communities, while Christian teaching gave them hope.

Leo I—justly called "the Great"—occupied the chair of Saint Peter during the darkest years of the fifth century, from 440 to 461. He was a man of powerful character, of rigid beliefs, of noble purpose, who had shown himself an able diplomatist with a firm grasp of political problems before he was elevated to the bishopric of Rome. As pope, he built up the spiritual supremacy of the Roman see and imposed unity of doctrine on a Church threatened with heresy and division. Through his vision and his achievement the Church survived the Dark Ages of barbarian rule as a civilizing force and the true heir in the West of Roman law and order.

The Huns were not the first barbarians to attack the Empire, neither were they the most dangerous. But they were the most alien and therefore the most terrifying. A nomadic people from the Steppes of Asia, with dark complexions, black hair, and squat, strong bodies, their chief occupation was hunting or fighting. They had no desire to settle. They did not seek (as some of the barbarians did) to become assimilated with the Roman people and to learn their skills. They continued heathen, hostile, interested only in plunder. They lacked any developed political sense and were divided into numerous rival bands, so that their brief period of power coincided with the reign of their only great leader, Attila. He had made himself sole king by murdering his brother, and during the twenty years of his reign (433–453) he compelled the lesser Hunnish chieftains to obey him and successfully asserted his rule over other barbarian tribes. His authority extended from the Danube and the Dniester to the Rhine.

The Roman Empire had experienced one last brief period of strength under the Spanish warrior Theodosius I (379–395). But on his death his dominions were divided between his two unimpressive sons, one ruling the East from Constantinople, the other ruling in the West. By the middle of the fifth century the Western Empire was crumbling fast. The Goths, who had sacked Rome in 410, were by now well-established in Gaul and Spain. The Vandals, crossing from Spain to Africa, had seized the rich province of the North African coast whence Rome had for centuries drawn her principal supply of grain.

The Huns, meanwhile, were encamped, rather than settled, on the Hungarian Plain. About the year 440 they began under Attila a series of devastating attacks on the Eastern Empire. The feeble Emperor Theodosius II sought to keep them out by paying a heavy annual tribute. Diplomatic exchanges of a kind thus grew up between the illiterate King of the Huns and the civilized, effete, imperial court. One Roman historian has left a detailed account of an embassy to Attila at his savage headquarters.

The sprawling "capital" of Attila's empire seems to have been somewhere near the modern Hungarian town of Jászberény. It was half village, half military camp, with turf huts and canvas tents roughly ranged in streets leading to the wooden residence of Attila. Only Attila, his principal wife, and a few of the greater chieftains lived in wooden houses, yet there was a stone-built Roman bath in the camp, the only luxury Attila seemed to think worth copying from the peoples he plundered and despised.

The Roman deputation was entertained at a banquet, where there was much drinking of healths and raucous merrymaking. But a strict if primitive formality hedged the person of Attila, who drank only from wooden vessels, ate only meat, and never smiled. Many of his warriors used gold and silver goblets, the loot of the imperial provinces, and had gems on their belts and sword hilts. But Attila to the end of his days affected the coarse and simple dress of a herdsman-warrior and scorned every luxury. He would not even eat bread—the food of peasants, unfit for a fighting man.

Short, swarthy, immensely broad-shouldered, with a flat nose and sparse beard, Attila seemed to Roman eyes scarcely human. But he bore himself with an air of formidable authority, even of majesty. His people feared him, but they also admired and trusted him, and looked up to him as one specially favored by their gods. His word was their law. The monkish chroniclers of later times enlarged on the ugliness, strangeness, and violence of this heathen people and their terrible king. After his death they named Attila the "scourge of God," sent down upon the decadent inhabitants of the Empire to chastise them for their vices.

The death of Theodosius II, and the accession of a more vigorous ruler at Constantinople, was the signal for Attila to turn his attention from the Eastern to the Western half of the Empire. In 451 he invaded Gaul. Checked at the battle of Châlons—it is usually so called, although the exact site is doubtful—Attila withdrew, but only to regroup his forces for a fresh attack.

In the spring of the following year, 452, he struck directly across the Alps into Italy, and claimed an imperial princess as his bride and a dowry of half the Empire. One of the ladies of the imperial house, in a moment of folly and frustration, does indeed seem to have sent him a ring and a letter. But it is probable that he used the incident merely as a pretext for an invasion that he would have undertaken in any case. The Huns needed warfare to keep them occupied; and Italy, under the rule of a weak and silly emperor, Valentinian III, was an obvious and easy prey.

The horde of Hunnish warriors swept down from the Alpine foothills, destroyed the great city of Aquileia, and ravaged the whole of the Lombardy Plain in the north. The wretched Emperor fled from his favorite residence at Ravenna to Rome, about three hundred miles away, and prepared to escape by sea. Rome itself, scarred from its capture by Alaric and the Goths forty years earlier, had no hope of rescue. Would Attila conclude what Alaric had begun? Would he utterly destroy the battered but still majestic city, the cradle of Empire and for centuries the ruler of the Western world?

The Roman Senate, the feeble bearers of a great tradition, sent a deputation to plead with Attila. It consisted of a one-time consul, Avienus, and the prefect of Italy, Trigetius. These titles had once meant power and authority; they were now empty echoes from the Roman past. Then, by popular outcry in the city, a third member was added to the deputation—Leo, the Bishop of Rome.

Leo was about sixty years of age. He had not won the respect and love of the Roman people by seeking popularity. In his sermons he castigated their vices and deplored their frenzied search for pleasure in the midst of disaster. But they admired his austerity and his strength, his rigid and uncompromising fidelity to what he believed. There was indeed a kind of resemblance between Leo and Attila. Saintly pope and heathen king were both men of formidable will who inspired reverence in their people.

After he became bishop of Rome in 440 Leo pursued two objectives—the establishment of Rome as the spiritual capital of Christendom and the consolidation of doctrine within the Church. He had now achieved both: the Emperor Valentinian III had confirmed the supremacy of the Roman see, and the Council of Chalcedon had established the central doctrine of the Incarnation according to the formula Leo had laid down. It was therefore with confidence in his achievements as well as faith in God that he set out to confront the King of the Huns.

What happened at the meeting? Why did Attila halt his advance and withdraw from Italy? Some historians have suggested that the Roman deputation persuaded the superstitious heathen that he would not survive the capture of Rome. Alaric had died within the year. Others argue, not unreasonably, that Attila would have retreated anyway. The season was already advanced, the resources of Italy were inadequate to feed his vast army, and it was his normal pattern of warfare to attack during the summer and fall back in the winter. The invasion would certainly have been renewed the next year had Attila lived to renew it. But he died that winter. On the night of his marriage to a new, young bride he burst a blood vessel and was found dead in the morning with the terrified girl crouching at his side.

Secular historians of all ages have tended to deny the significance of this meeting and to belittle the influence of the Pope. Yet the personality of Leo and his air of authority can hardly have failed to impress Attila and may have affected his decision. We shall never know. But we have evidence of another kind. Three years later, when Gaiseric the Vandal was at the gates of Rome, Leo went out to confront him as he had confronted Attila. No power on earth could have made the Vandal King relinquish his prey, yet Leo persuaded him to mitigate his violence, to spare the populace, not to burn the city, and to limit plundering to fourteen days. It was a modified deliverance, but it was a deliverance none the less, and the Romans blessed their dauntless pope for it.

Popular memory and ecclesiastical tradition, rightly remembering Pope Leo as a guardian and a deliverer, fastened on his confrontation of Attila as the symbol of his greatness. It is the idea and not the reality that matters. Leo did not, in the end, save Italy from conquest or Rome from capture. No man could have done that. He did something of more lasting consequence: he built the spiritual empire of the papacy on the ruins of imperial Rome. Without him the history of the barbarian invasions would not have been much different. But without him the history of medieval Christendom would have been wholly different. For he ensured the survival of the Church as an instrument of civilization.

So it came about that, more than a thousand years afterward, Raphael depicted the meeting of Leo with Attila to illustrate the spiritual triumph of the Church over physical force. In 1512 the theme had an additional appeal for his patron Pope Julius II. This warlike Renaissance pontiff had striven to free Italy from recurrent French invasion. "Out with the barbarians"—"*Fuori i barbari!*"—was a favorite political slogan of his: not a very flattering one to the French. How suitable, therefore, that Raphael should paint for him the expulsion of barbarians by a pope who became a saint, and should indeed plan to draw Julius himself in the part of Saint Leo.

Ironic fate decreed otherwise. Julius died before the picture was finished. His successor was the extravagant Medici prince who took the name of Leo X. Most generous of art patrons and most disastrous of popes, he came to impersonate his great namesake in Raphael's fresco. The artist has endowed the figure of the Pope with a calm majesty worthy of Saint Leo. But the face is not that of the strong-willed, single-minded architect of the Church. It is the puffy, self-indulgent face of Leo X. The upraised hand is not the lean and sinewy hand of the fearless priest who encountered Attila. It is the soft, white, well-manicured hand of a rich Renaissance epicure.

The incongruity of these details is scarcely noticeable in the general grandeur of Raphael's design. But later history was to add a further incongruity unknown to the painter. Leo the Great built up the spiritual power and unity of the Church. Leo X would live to face the challenge of Martin Luther, and to face it with such ineptitude, such lack of spiritual or political vision, that the unity of Western Christendom would be destroyed.

Miss Wedgwood, the author of The King's Peace *and* The King's War, *has made several notable contributions to* HORIZON, *including "The Prince of Patrons," for July, 1961.*

By ROBERT GRAVES

Pretense on Parnassus

"Nine-tenths of what passes as English poetry is a choice between vulgarity and banality." So says this English poet, taking aim at such eminent targets as Browning, Byron, Swinburne, and Kipling

$\mathbf{A}$ French editor invited me recently to join a symposium in praise of Robert Browning. At the risk of seeming a snob, I excused myself on the ground of his vulgarity: "This does not mean that Browning wrote in a nonacademic style for the larger public, but that he was clearly no gentleman. The Muse has, of course, shown equal favor to poets of every rank and condition: to King Henry VIII; to the Earl of Surrey; to Sir Walter Raleigh; to John Clare, the Northamptonshire peasant; to William Davies, the South Welsh tramp; to John Keats, whose father was a groom; and to William Shakespeare, whose father was a wholesale provision dealer. Therefore to call Browning clearly no gentleman, and seemingly introduce class barriers into a classless society, implies that he was clearly no poet either."

What *is* vulgarity? Ruskin defined it as a "deadness of heart and body resulting from prolonged, and especially from inherited, conditions of degeneracy." What he calls "vulgar" I should call "banal." There is a livelier, likable sort of vulgarity: the strident, active, healthy, uninhibited, generous vulgarity of the Edwardian music hall or of New York vaudeville when Teddy Roosevelt was President. But vulgarity as a critical term means, as a rule, someone's swaggering attempt to be at ease in a class or group with different customs and taboos from his own.

Vulgaritas carried no social stigma in ancient Rome, once the power of the aristocratic families had been broken. Gaius Petronius's Trimalchio was rich, insensitive, and uneducated; but as a priest of Augustus he felt thoroughly at ease in bullying and looking down on his better-bred and less successful fellow townsmen. Indeed, I read him as Petronius's satire on the Emperor Nero who, although brought up under the care of a barber and a Circus dancer, stood high above all social criticism. "Vulgarity," however, in English usage, is historically associated with *vulgus mobile,* "the easily moved crowd," from which comes the word "mob." The mob, or "mobility," were, for the three established "estates," rabble without patrons or clients, representation, responsibility, or convictions: the objects of scorn or pity.

Adult suffrage, two world wars, Labor governments, compulsory education, and crippling death-duties have gradually blurred social distinctions in Britain. Sportsmanship is now the one universally recognized moral virtue; all sportsmen rank as gentlemen. The servant class has disappeared; a skilled manual worker often earns more than a university graduate; and the diminished importance given to all but technical accomplishments in education encourages the spread of what used to be called "mob-taste" even among persons of royal blood. The *Daily Sketch* and *Daily Mirror* hail it as "the popular touch."

School anthologies harbor countless examples of vulgar verse, still fed to children as worthy of admiration. Take Browning's "Marching Along," his ballad about Kentish Sir Byng, a Cavalier who fought in the English Civil War. Browning, the son of a Bank of England clerk, was by birth and environment

Robert Browning: "his daydream of glory" was "undeniably vulgar." Not a true Cavalier, he was by birth really a "crop-headed Ironside."

an enthusiastic crop-headed Ironside. Yet here he casts himself for the part of a great-hearted, long-tressed Cavalier:

> *Kentish Sir Byng stood for his King,*
> *Bidding the crop-headed Parliament swing:*
> *And, pressing a troop unable to stoop*
> *And see the rogues flourish and honest folk droop,*
> *Marched them along, fifty-score strong,*
> *Great-hearted gentlemen, singing this song.*
>
> *God for King Charles! Pym and such carles*
> *To the Devil that prompts 'em their treasonous parles!*
> *Cavaliers up! Lips from the cup,*
> *Hands from the pasty, nor bite take nor sup*
> *Till you're—*
>
> CHORUS: *Marching along, fifty-score strong,*
> *Great-hearted gentlemen, singing this song.*

We read that Sir Byng pressed "great-hearted gentlemen" for the King's service. Browning used *pressed* because it has a more urgent sound than "raised," yet "pressing" implies forcibly overcoming their reluctance to serve the King—a trait, however, of which he reports them incapable. *Troop, stoop,* and *droop* all seem chosen to rhyme with each other, though *troop* probably occurred to Browning first. Being neither a soldier nor a historian, he did not know what strength a "troop" would have had in King Charles's day; but to glorify Sir Byng (a fictitious character, perhaps short for "Browning," and rhymed with *King*) he put it at one thousand Cavaliers, or two cavalry regiments. Sir Byng finds them all together by some happy accident, armed and accoutred, at a gigantic wine-and-pasty picnic. Before grace can be said, Sir Byng's apt rhyme about King Charles, Pym's carles, and their treasonous parles, provokes them to rise up, still hungry and thirsty, and march off to battle with no better preparation than a song. Talk of the Pied Piper of Hamelin! As the *Dictionary of National Biography* notes: ". . . his poems everywhere attest unflinching optimism." "Marching Along" is a daydream of glory, doubtless provoked (like the no less unhistorical "How They Brought the Good News from Ghent to Aix") by the sensuous rhythm of Browning's early-morning horseback constitutional in the park, and undeniably vulgar.

Here is Browning with his "Home-Thoughts from the Sea," a poem worked up from stray diary jottings:

> *Nobly, nobly Cape Saint Vincent to the North-west died away;*
> *Sunset ran, one glorious blood-red, reeking into Cadiz Bay;*
> *Bluish 'mid the burning water, full in face Trafalgar lay;*
> *In the dimmest North-east distance dawn'd Gibraltar grand and gray;*
> *"Here and here did England help me: how can I help England?"*
> *—say,*
> *Whoso turns as I, this evening, turn to God to praise and pray,*
> *While Jove's planet rises yonder, silent over Africa.*

Nine readers out of ten will identify *this evening* and *the burning water* with the sunset at Cadiz, supposing that Trafalgar lay on the Spanish coast opposite Cadiz Bay, Gibraltar to the northeast, where the dawn would presently break, and Cape St. Vincent some miles to the northwest. A glance at the map will surprise them: Cape St. Vincent lies one hundred and fifty miles almost due west from Cadiz; Trafalgar thirty miles south of Cadiz; and Gibraltar round the corner in the Mediterranean. Sentimental allusions to Nelson's victories at St. Vincent and Trafalgar and to Lord Heathfield's earlier defense of Gibraltar would, Browning reckoned, make patriotic schoolboys ambitious to join the Senior Service. The glorious blood-red sunset that reeked into Cadiz Bay is a daringly phrased reminder of Drake's surprise attack—against Royal orders—on the Spanish fleet in 1587. Needing a purple last line, Browning solemnly records that Jove's planet rose silent over Africay. Did he expect it to sing "Rule, Britanniay"?

But I should not like you to think that we English deduce Browning's vulgarity merely from his neglect of factual verisimilitude. What clinches it for us is his behavior when a mischief-maker reported to him an off-the-record comment by Edward FitzGerald (translator of Omar Khayyám) on the death of Elizabeth Barrett Browning: "No more *Aurora Leigh's*, thank God!" Instead of either scornfully dismissing this insult to his beloved wife's poetic masterpiece, or visiting FitzGerald with a horsewhip, as a gentleman of his day would have felt obliged to do, Browning wrote him a sonnet. He declared in it that he would not honor "good Fitz" by so much as spitting on him: "Spitting with lips once consecrated by hers."

Browning's vulgarity is a link between Thomas Campbell's and Rudyard Kipling's. Campbell, the youngest of an impoverished Scottish merchant's eleven children, won verse prizes at Glasgow University, and was "discovered" by the same Henry Mackenzie who had discovered Burns. "The Battle of Copenhagen," "Ye Mariners of England" (not Scotland), and other patriotic songs earned him a government pension. Though his hope of political advancement was frustrated by the death of his patron Fox, he lived comfortably from his patriotic verse throughout the Napoleonic Wars, and found it hard to make ends meet only during the long period of peace that followed Waterloo. Then he addressed his trumpet calls to other nations.

To the Greeks (1822):

> *Again to the battle, Achaians!*
> *Our hearts bid the tyrants defiance. . . . [sic]*

To the Spaniards (1823):

> How rings each sparkling Spanish brand!
> There's music in its rattle;
> And gay, as for a saraband,
> We gird us for the battle.
> Follow, follow!
> To the glorious revelry
> When the sabres bristle
> And the death-shots whistle.

While encouraging these Spaniards, was Campbell aware that the saraband is a slow, melancholy dance, most unsuitable for the gorgeous revelry of battle—its steps being two forward and three back? Did he even care?

To the Poles (1831):

> And have I lived to see thee, sword in hand
> Uprise again, immortal Polish land?

To the Germans (1832):

> The Spirit of Britannia
> Invokes across the main
> Her sister Alemannia
> To burst the tyrant's chain.

Campbell had served briefly as a volunteer when England's shores were threatened by Bonaparte, "But oh! what fagging work this volunteering is!" he wrote; and having had a grandstand view of real war at Ratisbon—from a monastery garden near the battlefield—he felt no inclination to go overseas. He confided to a friend, "I stood with the good monks of Saint James to overlook a charge of Kleinau's cavalry upon the French. This proved the most important epoch of my life in point of impressions, but they are so horrible to my memory that I study to banish them." Safe home, however, he could write:

> The combat deepens. On, ye brave
> Who rush to glory, or the grave!
> Wave, Munich! all thy banners wave,
> And charge with all thy chivalry!

Which reminds me of a vulgar old song:

> When the bugle calls we shall march to war
>   As we did in days gone by.
> When the bugle calls, we shall march, march, march,
>   April, May, June and July.
> When the bugle calls we shall march to war
>   And not a man will fear it—
> And I don't care how soon the bloody bugle calls,
>   So long as I don't hear it.

Campbell's "Wounded Hussar" had swept the country in 1799. A successful patriotic poem should have a long, rolling meter, with such feminine rhymes as *beaming–streaming, cherished–perished, story–glory;* and be utterly nonsensical in plot.

> Alone to the banks of the dark-rolling Danube
>   Fair Adelaide hied when the battle was o'er:
> "Oh, whither," she cried, "hast thou wandered, my lover?
>   Or here dost thou welter and bleed on the shore?

> "What voice did I hear? 'twas my Henry that sighed!"
>   All mournful she hastened; nor wandered she far,
> When, bleeding and low, on the heath she descried
>   By the light of the moon her poor wounded Hussar!

> From his bosom that heaved the last torrent was streaming,
>   And pale was his visage, deep marked with a scar!
> And dim was his eye, once expressively beaming,
>   That melted in love and that kindled in war!

For triumphs like this, Campbell was three times elected Rector of Glasgow University, and buried, on July 3, 1844, in Westminster Abbey, at the very center of Poets' Corner. Present were Lord Macaulay, John Gibson Lockhart, Lord Brougham, Sir Robert Peel, the Duke of Argyll, and a guard of grateful Polish nobles, one of whom sprinkled on the coffin a handful of earth from the grave of the patriot Kosciusko.

K ipling's uncertainty is explained by his sense of not-belonging—in an Anglo-Indian society where, as a Bombay-born journalist without either a settled English background or a university education, he ranked below the youngest second lieutenant in the tattiest battalion of the Indian Army. Worse, he was a Methodist, not Church of England. Yet Kipling had a quick journalistic eye and ear. Soon he revenged himself by interpreting British India to the stay-at-homes, with a good deal less sympathy for pukka sahibs than for Privates Mulvaney, Orth'ris and company, the regimental water-carrier Gunga Din, and the otherwise underprivileged. At the age of forty-one he was awarded the Nobel Prize. Kipling claimed to be a no-nonsense poet, a mouthpiece of the common people, who swept away academic humbug. His "Boots, boots, boots, boots!" is now the best-known English poem in the Soviet Union. But when the Establishment beckoned, he followed, at last squarely identifying himself with the Lords and Masters, rather than the "lesser breeds within the Law," and bravely shouldering the White Man's Burden.

Kipling became the unofficial poet laureate of the British Empire just before its liquidation. He missed the official appointment only because he had earned Queen Victoria's displeasure by alluding to her as "the Widow of Windsor." Like Browning

Rudyard Kipling: he "claimed to be a mouthpiece of the common people, but when the Establishment beckoned, he followed."

and Campbell, he weltered vicariously in gore, as in the climax to his fictional "Ballad of the *Clampherdown*":

> . . . *It was our war-ship* Clampherdown,
>   *Swung round upon the tide,*
> *Her two dumb guns glared south and north,*
> *And the blood and the bubbling steam ran forth,*
>   *And she ground the cruiser's side.*

> *"Captain, they cry, the fight is done,*
>   *"They bid you send your sword."*
> *And he answered: "Grapple her stern and bow.*
> *"They have asked for the steel. They shall have it now;*
>   *"Out cutlasses and board!"*

> *It was our war-ship* Clampherdown
>   *Spewed up four hundred men;*
> *And the scalded stokers yelped delight*
> *As they rolled in the waist and heard the fight*
>   *Stamp o'er their steel-walled pen.*

> *They cleared the cruiser end to end,*
>   *From conning-tower to hold.*
> *They fought as they fought in Nelson's fleet;*
> *They were stripped to the waist, they were bare to the feet,*
>   *As it was in the days of old.*

I could quote nothing from all English literature that transcended in vulgar bloody-mindedness the third of these stanzas. The stokers, no doubt ignoble lascars, unfit to wield a white man's cutlass, are left below decks; and their screams of pain as salt water reaches the boilers and steam scalds them are jovially interpreted as yelps of delight! *Bubbling,* by the way, has been transferred for the sake of euphony from *blood* to *steam.*

A frequent sign of poetic vulgarity is the use of Biblical language to heighten trivial passages. Kipling specialized not only in grandiose addresses to the Lord God of Hosts, but also in dewy-eyed quotations from the New Testament. The affected simplicity of "Gethsemane" shows him at his lowest:

> *The Garden called Gethsemane*
>   *In Picardy it was,*
> *And there the people came to see*
>   *The English soldiers pass.*
> *We used to pass—we used to pass*
>   *Or halt, as it might be,*
> *And ship our masks in case of gas*
>   *Beyond Gethsemane.*

> *The Garden called Gethsemane,*
>   *It held a pretty lass,*
> *But all the time she talked to me*
>   *I prayed my cup might pass.*
> *The officer sat on the chair,*
>   *The men lay on the grass,*
> *And all the time we halted there*
>   *I prayed my cup might pass.*

> *It didn't pass—it didn't pass—*
>   *It didn't pass from me.*
> *I drank it when we met the gas*
>   *Beyond Gethsemane.*

Why, at a period in the First World War subsequent to the issue of gas masks, as opposed to "respirators" (probably the early summer of 1916), Picardy peasants were still interested in watching the British soldiers pass, *or halt, as it might be;* and why they continued to occupy an area so close to the German lines that gas masks were habitually put on there; and why the pretty lass singled out this Christlike private soldier for her French monologue, when all he could do was lie on the grass in an agony, shut his eyes, and pray against gas; and why, for that matter, he *did* get gassed in the end—must remain mysteries. Perhaps the practical *Picardaise* wanted him to stop praying *un petit moment* and make sure that his mask had its eyepieces properly secured.

Nonscholarly pretense at scholarship is another form of poetic vulgarity, used throughout Browning's *Sordello,* though he quotes only the classics and a little Italian—not Chinese, Sanskrit, or Provencal, like his modernist successors of the Eliot-Pound school, who are as innocent of these tongues as President Eisenhower or Caroline Kennedy.

It is natural for young people to gather in a crowd, play the same games, use the same jargon; and if some physical misfortune or social disadvantage (rather than a rare extra gift of the spirit) differentiates one of them from his fellows, this often tempts him to some sort of megalomaniac overcompensation. Byron knew and regretted the colossal vulgarity that he shrouded by a cloak of aloof grandeur. It was a studious vulgarity: cosmetics and curlpapers tended his elegant beauty; an ingenious, though synthetic, verse technique smoothed his cynical Spenserian stanzas. But he had unexpectedly come into a peerage and an estate while still "wee Georgie Gordon with the feetsies"— whom his hysterical and unladylike mother used to send limping round the corner from her cheap Aberdeen lodgings to buy two-penny-worth of "blue ruin"; and whom, at the age of nine, a nymphomaniac Calvinist housemaid had violently debauched. His unease was prodigious. As he confesses in *Childe Harold*:

> *His [cup] had been quaffed too quickly, and he found*
>   *The dregs were wormwood; but he filled again,*
> *And from a purer fount, on holier ground,*
>   *And deemed its spring perpetual—but in vain!*
> *Still round him clung invisibly a chain*
>   *Which galled for ever, fettering though unseen,*

Lord Byron: "a studious vulgarity: an ingenious, though synthetic, verse technique smoothed his cynical Spenserian stanzas."

And heavy though it clanked not; worn with pain,
Which pined although it spoke not, and grew keen,
Entering with every step to look through many a scene.

Shelley noted in a letter to his friend Thomas Love Peacock: "Lord Byron is an exceedingly interesting person and, as such, is it not to be regretted that he is a slave to the vilest and most vulgar prejudices, and as mad as a hatter?" Byron adored no Muse, but acted as male Muse to scores of infatuated women who, like Lady Caroline Lamb, knew that he was "mad, bad, dangerous to know," adding: "His beautiful face is my fate." I pair Byron and Nero as the two most dangerously talented bounders of all time.

Swinburne's was an inverted vulgarity. His father had been an admiral, his grandfather an earl. After a healthy North Country childhood, he went on to Eton and Oxford. Later, he tried to edge, not into high society, but into the "fleshly" Bohemian set of pre-Raphaelite poets and painters. For them he celebrated the roses and raptures of vice; but whereas Byron could wearily boast of having enjoyed more than two hundred mistresses and scores of catamites, the impotent eroticism of Swinburne's verse, even when it celebrated merely vegetable Nature, leaves a worse taste in the mouth than *Childe Harold:*

BY THE NORTH SEA

A land that is lonelier than ruin;
  A sea that is stranger than death;
Far fields that a rose never blew in,
  Wan waste where the winds lack breath;
Waste endless and boundless and flowerless
  But of marsh-blossoms fruitless as free;
Where earth lies exhausted, as powerless
  To strive with the sea.

Far flickers the flight of the swallows,
  Far flutters the weft of the grass
Spun dense over desolate hollows
  More pale than the clouds as they pass;
Thick woven as the weft of a witch is
  Round the heart of a thrall that hath sinned,
Whose youth and the wrecks of its riches
  Are waifs on the wind.

Nineteenth-century poetic vulgarity is characterized by over-alliteration, ingenious rhymes—such as *blew in–ruin* and *riches–which is*—and a reckless disregard of prose sense. In Swinburne's windless, endless, boundless waste, the weft of grass, he says, fluttered far—spun dense over desolate hollows that were paler than the passing clouds, and thick woven as the weft of a witch around the heart of a sinner whose youthful charms had become like waifs in the wind. . . . But did a wind flutter the grass and drive the clouds, or did it not? And how can a waste region of England adjacent to the North Sea be endless and boundless? And how can a weft be *spun*? And if the grass had been spun densely over the desolate hollows, who could tell whether they

Charles Algernon Swinburne: his was "an inverted vulgarity." The son of an admiral and grandson of an earl, he "tried to edge into the Bohemian set."

were as pale as the clouds that passed? And how pale were the clouds, anyhow? And how thick a weft does a witch weave around the sinner's heart? And how do fruitless marsh-flowers spread themselves freely across the exhausted earth?

Keats, though no gentleman either by birth or education, had a genuine instinct for poetry and poetic principle; and the close attention he paid to craftsmanship made him recognize vulgarity in others and, as a rule, avoid it himself. He particularly lamented the fate of Burns: "Poor unfortunate fellow . . . how sad it is when a luxurious imagination is obliged, in self-defence, to deaden its delicacy in vulgarity and in things attainable, that it may not have leisure to go mad after things that are not." Vulgarity in religious dress is insidious; and Keats, who in this letter has been denouncing the hypocritical Kirk, was evidently referring to Burns's "Cotter's Saturday Night," an unco-guid set piece that contradicted his natural randiness and imitated Robert Fergusson's more authentic "The Farmer's Wife."

Almost every poet starts to write before finding his own voice, and puffs out his borrowed feathers. Every theatrical impersonation, every political, theological, or philosophical handout passed off as his own, is a vulgarity. The writing of true poems happens so unpredictably that the poet is beset by the temptation to write when not in the mood. He may think that this can be induced by withdrawing to a glade or quiet, book-filled study, or by violent adventure among corsairs, alguazils, Barmecides, and their modern equivalents. It cannot be.

No poet has yet solved the main problem: how to maintain the gift of certitude. Always to be in love; that is one recommendation. To treat money and fame with equal nonchalance is another. To remain independent is a third. To prize personal honor is a fourth. To make the English language one's constant study is a fifth. Yet lightning strikes where and when it wills. No one ever knows. It is easy to take up a pen at random and plead: "I'm just keeping my hand in." But nine-tenths of what passes as English poetry is the product of either careerism or keeping one's hand in: a choice between vulgarity and banality.

As the elected Professor of Poetry at Oxford University, Robert Graves is called on to deliver an annual series of lectures. This article was adapted from one of his most recent, as was "The Poet in a Valley of Dry Bones" in the March, 1963, issue of HORIZON.

By HENRY ANATOLE GRUNWALD

AN ADDRESS FROM THE CLASS OF 1944

The way to begin a sermon is to find a text, and the same goes for a commencement address. I can think of no better text than some lines from W. H. Auden's Phi Beta Kappa poem, which he delivered at Harvard shortly after World War II. He called it "Under Which Lyre—A Reactionary Tract for the Times," and in it he described a college generation rent by the struggle between the followers of Apollo and Hermes, between the pompous, humorless, earnestly ambitious and the playful, disorganized, rebelliously bright. There was no doubt on whose side Auden ranked himself as he stated his Hermetic Decalogue:

> *Thou shalt not do as the dean pleases,*
> *Thou shalt not write thy doctor's thesis*
> > *On education*
> *Thou shalt not worship projects nor*
> *Shalt thou or thine bow down before*
> > *Administration.*
>
> *Thou shalt not answer questionnaires*
> *Or quizzes upon World-Affairs,*
> > *Nor with compliance*
> *Take any test. Thou shalt not sit*
> *With statisticians nor commit*
> > *A social science.*
>
> *Thou shalt not be on friendly terms*
> *With guys in advertising firms,*
> > *Nor speak with such*
> *As read the Bible for its prose,*
> *Nor, above all, make love to those*
> > *Who wash too much.*
>
> *Thou shalt not live within thy means*
> *Nor on plain water and raw greens.*
> > *If thou must choose*
> *Between the chances, choose the odd;*
> *Read* The New Yorker, *trust in God;*
> > *And take short views.*

TO THE CLASS OF 1963

*Will the new generation
be called Silent, Committed,
Cautious, Explosive, or
all four at once?*

In brief, the poet who named the Age of Anxiety was now warning against the Age of Conformity. The contents of conformity change; reading *The New Yorker,* for instance, has by now become a conformist act. But Auden's lines are characteristic of what has been said about you, the younger generation, for many years. It was said that you always did what the dean pleases. That you eagerly bowed down to Administration. That you actually enjoyed projects, and that you took your tests—as well as your trials—with compliance. That you were quite ready to live within your means and that, if you were not actually on friendly terms with guys in advertising firms, you wanted to be. In short, that you didn't raise enough hell, that you were too quiet, too well-behaved. You were called the Silent Generation, the Cautious or Conservative Generation, the Brainwashed Generation, even the Non-generation, in the sense that you supposedly had no collective identity at all.

It was said that you had no heroes and no villains, that you had no axes to grind—all your axes had turned into buried hatchets. It was said that you were not interested in politics or in causes. It was said that you were earnest and dull. "They speak," said one writer, "in tones Univac might adopt while addressing a mimeographing machine."

Surveying the college students of the late fifties, and that very nearly includes you, David Riesman found the young yearning to belong to nice, large organizations, and at the same time to escape from bigness into the "post-collegiate fraternity of the small suburb." W. H. Whyte found you to be embryonic organization men; the young, he said, "do not wish to protest, they wish to collaborate." "Sometimes," wrote Wallace Stegner, "a professor is baited into protest by the rows and circles of their closed, watchful, apparently apathetic faces and says, 'My God, feel something! Get enthusiastic about something, plunge, look alive, go boom!'"

Lately some of these views have changed, and it has been decided in certain quarters that you go boom, after all. The

*An annual ritual is enacted by undergraduates (rear) and
graduate students (shifting hoods) at Georgetown University.*

Silent Generation, it was announced, had found its voice. You have begun to march, to protest, to rebel. There is talk of the Explosive Generation, the Committed Generation, the Upbeat Generation. A popular magazine extravagantly reported that there had not been so much "youth activity" since the Children's Crusade in 1212 (conveniently forgetting the disastrous end of that pathetic event). Yet even as your new rebelliousness was reported, some doubts remained. One professor not long ago noted that you keep your dissents out of sight, that you "wear a mask." And a New York newspaper recently found that when you protest, you do so without banners; and that, "Freud-conditioned," you strive for adjustment rather than adventure.

When the older generation urges the younger generation to raise more hell rather than pleading with it to calm down, we have a strange reversal of a traditional human situation, suggesting that something important is afoot. A parallel comes to mind. The young people who grew up after the Napoleonic wars were distinctly world-weary, bored with politics, bored with causes, apparently stifled by an era of artificial peace, melancholy and, to begin with, silent. Meanwhile the older generation yearned for the glories, whether tricolored or royal blue, of yesteryear. One can imagine how they must have deplored the listlessness and dullness and morbidity of the younger generation. Yet we know that this younger generation in short order was to burst out with a major revolution in the arts and in philosophy, the revolution we call Romanticism. Historical parallels are feeble bridges and I don't want to overload this one, except to suggest that today, also, appearances are deceiving—and that today, also, more is going on than meets the eye.

When you reach a certain age—for instance my age or the age of most of your critics—you will find that you want to see your own youth reflected in the rising generation. What seems to disturb us about you is that you are so different from what we were like at your age, or at least what we *think* we were like. My own generation grew up in the thirties, and we were in college during the backwash of the thirties. We certainly did not think of ourselves as conformist or quiet. But our world was as simple as a melodrama. It had certain clearly defined villains: the fascists abroad, the reactionaries at home and, to some of us, the capitalists anywhere. Our world also had clearly defined heroes—the liberals and reformers, whether in politics or in culture. Some of us had a kind of know-nothing distrust of all isms; some of us were isolationists in foreign affairs as well as in ideology. But by and large we shared a great belief in the perfectibility of society. The time was out of joint, oh curséd spite—but we were sure we had been born to set it right. And so we signed manifestoes, made speeches, joined clubs, fought crusades, glorified the literary or artistic or political rebels.

But were we really a rebellious generation? Not at all. We were conformists of revolution, of stale revolution. We conformed to the rebellious attitudes that were then fashionable, to a whole set of supposedly progressive and liberal ideas that had been handed to us by older teachers, older writers, older brothers—or, should I say, by Big Brother. We were in the grip of what Sidney Hook has called ritualistic liberalism. We chanted the rituals, often without knowing what they meant, and we were brutally pedantic in correcting anyone who deviated from the accepted text. We sneered at Babbitts whom we had never met; we cheered for proletarians whom we had never known. What a warm, homey, sheltered feeling it used to be to sit with a bunch of like-minded fellows and mouth the clichés of Marxism—or of abstract art, or of psychoanalysis—and feel righteously revolutionary and daring at the same time. Our gestures, even our despair or our anger, were not original. We were told by others: "Come on in—the wasteland is fine." We were not a lost generation; we had been handed detailed instructions, with maps, on how to get lost.

And that, I think, is the way you differ from us. With some notable exceptions, you don't seem to be given to the sweeping generalization, the broad cause, the all-purpose rebellion. Someone has called you a generation of private seekers; perhaps you are also a generation of private rebels. Some of you, of course, are merely conformists in reverse; you automatically reject everything that is In and automatically embrace everything that is Out. But on the whole, there are signs that you use your own judgment more sharply than we did and that you are closer to reality than to slogans.

*H*ow did this difference come about? You can take your choice of several explanations—the sobering effects of war and the Bomb, the lulling absence of a Depression. But beyond all this, I believe that we have gone through a very basic change, through one of those times when the ground on which we stand shifts under our feet. Whatever our politics may have been, the large majority of us back in our college years shared a philosophy, a vision of man in this world. Human beings, let alone a whole generation, never really fit a pattern. But in a broad sense, I think I can describe our philosophy.

For one thing, we were pragmatists. We eagerly pounced on the notion that philosophy and ethics must be subject to practical tests—"must work." Whatever the merits of pragmatic philosophy, we used it chiefly to confirm our whims and prejudices and to reject anything we found uncomfortable because it claimed to be a permanent principle, whether the categorical imperative or the moral law or merely the greatest good for the greatest number.

We were relativists. We were sure that good and evil, right and wrong, were variable, indeed little more than fashions that changed with time and place. As Ronald Knox put it, "I believe" was replaced by "I feel." Any notion of unchanging values shocked and angered us. Indeed, the Absolute was our Devil; and when we came across it, we mumbled rapid incantations to Saint John Dewey.

We were, in a sense, logical positivists, although that organized suicide of philosophy did not really become fashionable until some years later. Still, we were at one with those who insist that philosophy must concern itself only with semantics, with working out precise communication, and not with values. One of the lasting memories I brought away from college concerns a coed whose name I don't recall and whose face is now only a vague blur, but who will be forever in my mind. She used to sit in class, carefully listening to the talk, and whenever someone said something—I mean, actually *said* something—she would rise and thunder her condemnation, the most devastating thing she could utter: "But now you are making a value judgment!"

We were skeptics, of course. Essentially, we distrusted religion. And above all, we were determinists. We believed that man was merely the product of his environment, his physical, social, historical, and psychological environment; and that if you could change his environment, you could change man. In line with that we were ready—in Auden's phrase—to commit a social science, any social science. We believed, with a long line of thinkers—including in their very different ways Auguste Comte and Herbert Spencer and Dewey—that scientific principles could and must be applied to shaping man's life. We believed in human engineering, in social air-conditioning.

I believe you recognize these attitudes, because they persist today. You share many of them. And yet I believe that you, and we, have begun to question them.

Pragmatism is not dead, and probably never will be. It is deeply embedded in the American tradition. It has given us glories along with disasters. But I think we have come to see that the question Does it work? is not the ultimate question in life.

Relativism is with us, and always will be. It is wise to recognize the ever-fluctuating meanings that mankind assigns to good and evil. And yet I think we have come to know more deeply than before that some things—such as the existence of a moral sense in man—are above change.

As to positivism, I think we are inclined once again to realize that philosophy's task is not semantics but the approach to wisdom, that to make "value judgments" is what we have a mind for. As to religion, I think we are more apt to recognize that most skepticism is insufferably shallow or, at the very least, that religion may once more be discussed in polite intellectual society. As for determinism, we are still fascinated, and at times hypnotized, by questions of environment, but I think we have also come to realize there is more to man than the sum of the forces that work on him.

Apart from history, apart from reason and intuition, it was science itself that helped us to see this. For where science was once glibly regarded as the answer to all mysteries, it is now more likely to be seen as deepening the mystery.

Physics, once as solid and simple as Newton's apple, has just about dissolved matter. Mathematics, once cold and beautiful and terrestrial, has taken off into infinity and very nearly into metaphysics. Medicine, which not long ago regarded the human body merely as a flesh-and-blood machine, today speaks of psychological influences and of psychosomatic disturbances that reassert mind over matter—and that very nearly recall medieval beliefs of possession by evil spirits. The great new would-be science of psychoanalysis, which is really an art, almost a form of poetry, has contributed to all this. It has led us, possibly against its intention, to the rediscovery of the soul, a concept that in my day was considered as old-fashioned as the crinoline.

In other words we know—and you know—that man is not so simple as we used to think. I believe you are slowly, gradually, rediscovering people in all their complexity, weakness, and greatness.

*B*ut where that rediscovery is leading, we cannot tell. To be frank about it, we do not really know you very well— and there may be more involved here than the usual awkward lack of communication between generations. Even the terms in which we insist on speaking of you—rebellion and conformity—may not really fit your own private dictionaries. For sometimes it seems that you do not so much rebel or conform as ignore; you do not struggle against the *status quo*, nor join it, but you bypass it.

Is it, among other reasons, because you sense yourselves to be living in a vitally different age from ours? Is it that our attitudes, our watchwords, and our hopefully offered solutions—or half-solutions—seem beside the point to you? And could it be that the change in atmosphere dates from Hiroshima? If so, you will sooner or later come up against the fact that the human condition does not truly change through plague, famine, progress, reaction, disaster, war, and even the possibility of total extinction. But how that human condition really strikes you is still a puzzle. You somehow seem a little withdrawn, a little alienated—members of that "inner emigration" which has seemed so often characteristic of twentieth-century man. As you work, play, read, and prepare for careers, are you really passive resisters? Despite your occasional protest marches or manifestoes, are you really unconcerned about the dilemmas and challenges of society? Or have you found your own way of coping with them?

If so—and there are many of us who believe you have— you are keeping the secret. Perhaps you cannot quite articulate what you have found that makes the old patterns, even the old patterns of youth and age, rebellion and conformity, seem irrelevant to you. Perhaps even if you could articulate it, we would not believe you. But we are wondering.

Mr. Grunwald, a senior editor of Time, *writes frequently for* HORIZON. *In March his subject was utopias past and present.*

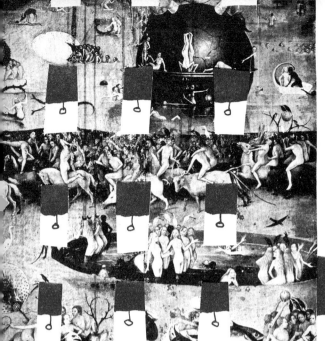

CHARMATZ

MONDRIAN IS
A PAPER NAPKIN

Now that America's all out for art,
Brancusi will be a doorknob

THE BOSCH

Art has won the race, all right—the race for the most effective status symbol of the year. It has left the competition (music, literature, and English accents) far behind. In Manhattan alone there are three apartment houses named for artists: The Rembrandt, The Van Gogh, and The Picasso. There is as yet no Hotel Stravinsky, no Robert Frost House. As for me, I don't think I'll move till someone builds The Hieronymus Bosch—that's what I would call an Address.

The urge to culture has brought art out of palace and cathedral and into our world: bank and coffeehouse—into our whole world, even the barbershops and the shoe salons. And into my favorite counter lunch uptown, which already had glamour enough for hamburgers and cole slaw. The counter seats were shrimp and turquoise; the walls were flecked with gold. The slaw was delicious. Then the place elevated its tone by adding paintings. There was something about those gold-flecked walls around my one-quarter-pound, all-beef burger-on-a-bun. There is something else about these paintings. Had they been Raphaels, they couldn't have made a Pavillon of a sandwich joint. Confidentially, there's not a Raphael in the lot. The place is just a sandwich joint with bad paintings.

A dress shop that sells Greenwich Village off-beat chic to Fifth Avenue recently advertised "Sculpture in the Fifth Avenue gallery." Since my imagination couldn't stretch beyond mannequins and dressmakers' dummies, I went down to check. When I couldn't find the gallery inside, I looked in the window, and there it was: several small abstract sculptures, even a tiny painting, all tastefully arranged amid scarfs and belts and beads. It made me think of those twenty-three-volume encyclopedias in my grocery store. I've never tried to read the encyclopedia between the catsup and the cans of beer, but I did have some trouble contemplating those statues while easing a dress down over my brand-new eight-dollar hairdo.

In the poshest lingerie showroom in Manhattan, a welded metal sculpture sits on the three-ply carpet. On this particular sculpture, Model #3015 bandeau brassière dangles from one spiky arm; Model #6124 drapes garters over another. Display techniques have reached a new level. Wait till the Chase Manhattan commissions a money tree.

Simply putting more art in more places will not make aesthetes of us all. Whistler said, "A life passed among pictures makes not a painter—else the policeman in the National Gallery might assert himself."

In the new art movement, art is the prime decoration. Wall-to-wall art is better than wall-to-wall carpeting. Look at what has happened to apartment lobbies. Every new apartment lobby with any genuine pretension is tastefully decked out in canvas and bronze. It used to be that wood paneling, fireplaces, and provincial chairs reassured us downstairs about the residents upstairs. New we get yards of paint and scraps of welded metal. I confess that I often prefer my own lobby, where a turquoise leather couch faces a brown tweed couch over a red rug and under gray curtains; it doesn't exactly have everyday chic, but at least its ugliness is honest. What committee chooses lobby art anyway? What I have seen won't keep me interested long enough to pass the time till the elevator comes. It's orphan art; nobody loves it and nobody wants it for itself.

As the decorator's darling, art sometimes suffers from misguided affection. Not so very long ago a noted decorator commissioned a painting for a client. She sent the artist a swatch of blue wool chenille, a swatch of bluer velvet, a snip of pink brocade, and a dab of plum jelly. "These are the colors in the living room," she wrote. "Please incorporate them in the painting; it will pull the room together." She chose the wrong artist, of course. The right one would have incorporated the swatches in the painting, and no doubt the jelly. Another

By VICKI GOLDBERG

decorator I know designed a pink and beige boudoir around a magnificent pink and beige Braque, effectively reducing the Braque to a feminine exercise in taste—if you could tell where the painting stopped and the room began.

The little decorator touches are occasionally more important than the art. There is the real-life lady who walked into a gallery famed for its impressionists and asked for something blue to go with her green rug. Then there are decorator groupings of paintings. A friend of mine has five paintings in a group on one side of her fireplace, none on the other. It's not a matter of space; she must like the pattern better than the paintings. I liked it, too. But I can't recall a single picture. Living with art must be like living with a man; you are supposed to respect it, not subdue it.

In the expanding world of art, reproductions pose a special problem, if only because of their numbers. The productive capacities of an offset press make Picasso look like a piker, although both press and painter are turning out Picassos; and the spread of what Madison Avenue would call art's image, through art books and cheap copies, raises the problem of knowing art at one remove only. The new and awkward dilemma is that of the tourist who is appalled to find Rodin's *Thinker* too large; it simply doesn't match the compact energy of the faithful reproduction on his desk.

What is glorious about art as a badge of culture is that it is so democratic. Reproductions, after all, cost next to nothing. Like the real McCoy, though on a more modest level, they play an important role in the cultural pecking order. A grand delicatessen in Westport, Connecticut, hangs Modiglianis above the pickle barrel, Gauguin beside the hot pastrami. Westport, of course, is that kind of town.

Mike Nichols and Elaine May do a skit about a suburbanite coming home and speaking to his wife (off stage) about the usual things: the commuter train, the club car, where's my Martini, and how's the baby's cold. When the wife comes on stage, he draws back aghast, murmurs "I must be in the wrong house," and dashes out. I picture the house as a *House and Garden* home in a *New Yorker* cartoon, the walnut shelves topped by one of those caky plaster heads of Nefertiti that are advertised in the Sunday book section—one in every home in the development. You'd think the Organization Man would prize original art as one of the few areas where the unique is still available, standing as he does by the pit of conformity that yawns at his feet.

Art is not just more numerous; it is growing bigger, too, just like books and movies and children on vitamin drops. Since apartments are shrinking, paintings often have to be used as room dividers. One wealthy collector has two room-divider paintings in one large room. The place looks like a fancy labyrinth for rich rats. We seem to have an urge toward more than one of a kind—two cars, two TV's, and a phone where *you* are at the moment, in color, of course. Now we are reproducing art in enough different ways to give ordinary households museum status. Raphael drawings turn up on boxes that hide cigarettes and Titians on matchbooks that light them. Satyrs copied from old prints chase nymphs around the wastebasket. The Louvre is practically catalogued on one plastic shower curtain that sells at a minimal price for so much art, and art appears in the backgrounds of magazine ads, most often behind ladies poised on elegant staircases above gentlemen in tails and bourbon.

Last night I had a nightmare. I was in a strange house. As I reached for the door, my hand clasped the cool, ovoid head of Brancusi's *Muse* on one end of a Yale lock. "Brancusi is a doorknob," I muttered, and woke up. Any why not? A painting by Paul Klee has been reproduced in vinyl flooring, lovingly lavished on a lady's dressing room in a model apartment. Brancusi may not be a doorknob, but Leonardo is a dish towel since the *Mona Lisa* hit Washington, D.C. Mondrian is a paper cocktail napkin and matching coasters, available in department stores for a dollar plus tax. Mondrian is also a beaded curtain, "suitable for room dividers." And Mondrian, in the guise of a cotton blouse on a large girl's back, could recently be seen eyeing Mondrian, in the guise of a painting, at the Museum of Modern Art.

The possibilities of reproducing art on paper goods are enormous, and certainly simpler than creating new designs. A roll of paper towels could constitute an entire art history, detachable at every phase. It is supposed to be good for the economy to invent new ways to waste things, and profitable to invent them beautifully. But I'd rather not drown the *Mona Lisa* every time I dry the dishes. Lord knows I already find it hard enough to hear the "William Tell Overture" without yelling "Hiyo, Silver, away!" Now when I see a Mondrian, will I always hear in my mind's ear the gentle clink of ice cubes in a highball glass?

My cousin Andy, twice removed, has a mind completely uncluttered with art. But he wanted to see New York's two-million-dollar Rembrandt, so I trundled him off to the Metropolitan Museum. Andy looked at the painting, his eyes brimming over with money. "I like Van Gogh better," he announced. "You know, the guy that cut off his ear."

It occurred to me, fleetingly, that perhaps art has been popularized a bit too rapidly. No one ever said to me, "Shakespeare, the guy that willed his wife the second-best bed," or "Schumann, the guy that went to court to get a bride." Art's enormous popularity is, after all, relatively recent. Attendance at the Metropolitan Museum climbed from 900,000 in 1940 to two million in 1950, almost three million in 1960, and four million in 1961, a growth rate well ahead of the census. Perhaps we ought to practice art control? Or perhaps someday we might institute better art history courses under competent supervision in the public schools, use television as a popular teaching medium for art (as Britain has), and apply principles of good design to our buildings, our cities, and all the objects that surround us. Then, perhaps, we'd respect art too highly to wear it as a mere badge of culture; for then, undoubtedly, "We'd all love art in a seemly way/With an earnest soul and a capital A."

Mrs. Goldberg, who views this subject as a graduate student in the fine arts, lives in New York with her husband and two sons.

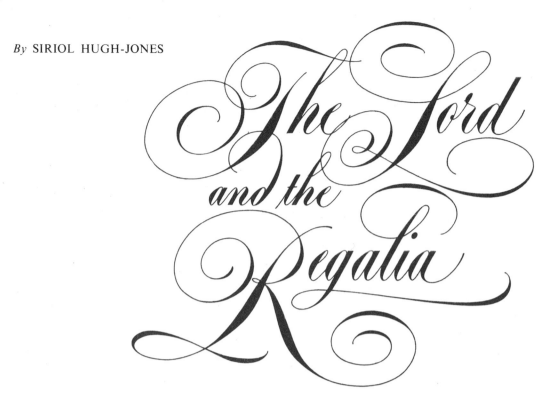

By SIRIOL HUGH-JONES

The Lord and the Regalia

His full name is Baron Twining of Tanganyika and Godalming. He has served Britain as soldier and proconsul, and has now written *the* book about crown jewels. His friends call him "Twinks"

Crowns of gold have a potent and conditioning magic. Spellbinding and hierarchical, they glitter darkly through nurseries and schoolrooms, identifying the boss man at first glance. "Hans entered, and the good old King came forward to meet him, wearing his dressing gown and embroidered slippers, yet with his gold crown on his head, and holding in one hand the sceptre, in the other the orb, the symbols of kingly power. . . ." From fairy stories we press on to Shakespeare, where reigning Monarchs, Usurpers, and Heirs Apparent devote powerful speeches to the Crown's mystery, hand the thing back and forth, grab it from sleeping brothers, and brood beautifully about its sacred responsibilities. Every child knows that if in the thick of battle you find the crown hanging carelessly upon a thornbush, the thing to do is fit it firmly and instantly over your own helmet. Every child, possibly even Oliver Cromwell, at about four puts a pudding basin on his head, takes a stout grip on a wooden mixing spoon, says "Look, I'm the King," and is never quite the same again.

There should therefore be a ready-made market for an astonishing volume recently published in England by the firm of B. T. Batsford, called *A History of the Crown Jewels of Europe* and priced at ten guineas. In 707 enormous pages the book gives a thorough and detailed account of regalia and crown jewels in twenty-six European countries over seventeen centuries. There are 230 pages of illustrations, and "information is given," says the jacket in the crisp, level tone of simply letting facts speak for themselves, "on over 600 crowns, 187 sceptres, 98 orbs and 116 ceremonial swords." It weighs eight and three-quarter pounds, and would look at home chained to a lectern; it faintly gives one the feeling that the most respectful and indeed perhaps the easiest

way to read it would be standing up. If ever a book could justly be called king-sized, this is it.

The author of this majestic and breathtaking work is a burly, ebullient peer named Edward Francis Twining, who in 1958 was sonorously created Baron Twining of Tanganyika and of Godalming. (Godalming is a nice modest place, a small town in the London dormitory belt with virtually nothing remarkable about it, and one rather loves Lord Twining for having linked it so majestically and euphoniously with Tanganyika.) He has won honor and high regard in a world where it might be unexpected, to say the least, to come across the compiler of a history of regalia. Born in 1899, he is the son of a clergyman and was educated at Lancing College and the Royal Military College, Sandhurst. He was a military man until 1929, when he began a career in colonial government which culminated in a remarkable nine-year term as Governor and Commander-in-Chief of Tanganyika Territory. There he worked strongly toward racial parity, was loved and respected, and exercised a guidance both energetic and enlightened.

Lord Twining is held by some to look a little like the late Charles Laughton, and in the courtly words of *The Times* "still preserves the Regular Officer's command of blistering invective." A man of abundant vitality, he seems to have a talent for the unexpected and unpompous not quite pronounced enough to be called eccentric. On a flying visit home from Borneo, where he was first governor and then commander-in-chief, he asked the Colonial Office for a supply of trained hawks to police the Borneo rice fields and announced his intention of promoting two new export industries—the supply of orchids to America and edible

An author in full dress: ending a term as Governor of Tanganyika in 1958, Sir Edward Twining—
soon to be made a peer—bids "Kwaheri" (farewell) to Her Majesty's faithful subjects there.

birds' nests to China. At a Government House fete at Dar-es-Salaam he balanced an apple on the head of Lady Twining and permitted a schoolgirl to shoot at it with bow and arrow. In Tanganyika they asked earnestly for his period of office to be extended; and when he said goodbye to tribesmen in Lake Province, he put on an imposing feather headdress and danced with the rest. Thirty years ago in Uganda at a small informal dinner party he sang "Call out the Army and the Navy" and "There Was a Boy Whose Name Was Jim" by Hilaire Belloc, in Swahili. His dearest friends are said to call him Twinks, and such a sprightly nickname seems suitable.

Lord Twining's character may perhaps be described as enormously, exuberantly English—in the manner that the English themselves most like to think of as the essence of their national nature. Very English, too, is the unexpected taste for the sort of "hobby activity" one wouldn't have dreamed of, and that grew to mammoth size (you find the same sort of thing in generals who appear—or like to appear—to soldier brilliantly but do so absent-mindedly while devoting the bulk of their time and energies to bird-watching or making poetry anthologies), combined with the practical, down-to-earth common sense acquired during administrative experience in the field. A request for hawks may look picturesque in retrospect, but one may be sure that at the time it was the best way of keeping rice fields clear of marauders.

The surprising, endearing, and self-effacing administrator-encyclopedist says characteristically of his book, "There are one or two stories—of my own invention—as to how I started on this venture. They are purely apocryphal." In fact Lord Twining began in 1930, when he was administering a remote subdistrict in

Uganda about the size of Wales. "Absorbing as the local problems were, one found oneself starved of any intellectual relaxations and felt the need for a hobby to act as a foil." He had always been interested in history and traditional State ceremonial, and references to European regalia in three or four different books and papers he happened to be reading at the time "sparked off the idea." The Director of Geological Survey sent him a small collection of books on gem stones, and the whole vast project took root. ("Little did I realize at the time," he writes mildly, "the immensity of the task.")

*P*eriodic long leaves afforded opportunities to stop off here and there for firsthand research—he lists Rome, Vienna, Prague, and Cracow—and this "enabled me to begin to understand the scope of the subject." His research methods in the early days were again both characteristic and common-sensible. "Not knowing any Kings or Queens myself, I wrote to Thos. Cook and Son and they were most helpful in getting me into backroom collections not open to the public." He collected an extensive library, more than four thousand photographs, and a small army of translators covering between them some twenty languages.

"In the course of time," writes Lord Twining, who was meanwhile nothing if not fully occupied with public affairs, "I really became quite knowledgeable on my subject, and nothing gave me greater pleasure than to tell curators that they had items of great historical value tucked away in their cupboards about which they were unaware. True, my joke sometimes misfired, but it was astonishing what was revealed. This gave me a lumber-room complex and I am convinced that priceless treasures are lying moldering in lumber rooms, put away and forgotten."

Lord Twining's lifelong treasure hunt sometimes brought him curious problems in procedure. Obstacles only spurred him into more forceful and inventive action, or, in his own words, "where one came up against the greatest difficulties, the greater the kick one got out of it when one overcame them." For more than thirty years Lord Twining gathered material and drafted chapters, giving the work "an hour or two of my spare time when the spirit moved me." During his leaves, he checked information by visits to one hundred twenty museums, treasuries, collections, churches, and palaces in seventy different places in twenty-five countries, Russia and Spain being the only two he did not visit himself. The whole monumental task was not completed until after his retirement in 1958.

A History of the Crown Jewels of Europe is arranged according to a simple alphabetical plan, beginning with Austria and ending with Yugoslavia, with a chapter for each country and one for the Holy See. At the end of each chapter Lord Twining has been thoughtful enough to help out shaky historians by adding a roll call of kings with their relevant dates. (And I would challenge any non-historian to feel secure on the running order of, say, Childeric the Stupid, Pepin the Short, and Charles the Fat, or to sort out the Louis' who were variously the Debonair, the Stammerer, the Indolent, and the Quarreler.)

Through the book run several major themes, haunting and ominous, though never directly stated. One is power, as the stylized playing-card figures of kings and queens succeed and die, are deposed, intermarry, enlarge their territories, put their second-best crowns into pawn, and dazzle the eyes of awe-struck enemies by a sensational display of diamonds. Another is money—the treasures and gems that were used to strike bargains and seal treaties, that were looted and stolen and moved hurriedly in insignificant little boxes during revolutions, that were acquired by penny-wise royal mistresses with a gift for sticking it out, and grabbed back by royal wives, that were thrown out of windows and grubbed for in the gravel, that were once set around miniatures of loved faces and made into pretty little earrings and bow brooches, and later sold at auction to dealers and collectors. A third is the irony of changing fortune, especially when kings, who were often dangerously mortal, and stones, which are tough and coveted, are the links in the main chain of narrative. A stone can go from an Oriental prince's turban to a crown to a ring to a cloak clasp to a brooch to a sword hilt; it can be cleft and cut and reset according to the fashion and the growing skill of jewelers and, when the royal cards are packed away in the box, finish up in a State museum. Jewels may be worn as symbols of inherited trust and power; they may add pomp to a State occasion designed to impress, or may disguise an empty treasury by presenting a bold face to the world; or they may serve simply to pretty up a plain and insignificant royal personage and make a handsome one look like something out of another and far, far better world.

A history of the crown jewels of Europe is necessarily a history of European monarchies as well, and Lord Twining's interest is not specifically in jewelry and precious stones but, as he says himself, in "the historical and symbolic attributes of these objects." Nevertheless, by the end of the twenty-seven vast collections, it is hard not to feel just faintly puritan about these preeminent persons' need to amass such a stunning quantity of diadems, jeweled girdles, blazing buttons, diamond-dripping earrings, and great waterfall-necklaces, so that barely a square inch of themselves remained to be covered by mere silk and velvet. The beautiful stark burial crowns of early Germany and Hungary, old gray wolves of crowns, looking as though they were made for heroic warrior kings, come as an extraordinary relief; and one's heart warms toward ugly, witty Louis XI of France, who may have made his coronation entry in style with jewels worth a million *écus* on his horse's harness alone, but who for everyday wear preferred an old felt hat decorated with a small leaden saint, and chose to go to his grave very plain indeed. It is perhaps something similar that makes the four early Russian crowns now in the Kremlin Museum look so extraordinarily elegant and appealing. They are like four small, jeweled cathedral domes sitting snugly in four wide bands of fur. To all intents and purposes they are in fact fur hats. They are practical, sensible even, in spite of the grandeur; cozy crowns for cold-weather kings.

*L*ord Twining maintains that there is no such thing as a "best" collection, though he reckons the British and Russian crown jewels to be the most valuable and the Bohemian regalia to have special artistic merit. England, being the only country where the coronation service still survives and kings and queens are entitled to wear the royal crown, has a fine fat chapter with its pages literally glowing with crowns, many of which, to the inexperienced eye, look like overstuffed pincushions. And some have a curiously stagey, theatrical look, as if worn in a tuppence colored print by David Garrick as Richard III.

Norman kings made a practice of holding three public crown-wearings each year, but Edward I gave it up because he hated wearing his crown in public. Richard I, who was no lightweight, had to have his coronation crown supported by two earls and hastily changed into something less burdensome before leaving the church, thereby setting a useful precedent. Lord Twining stoutly disbelieves any suggestion that King John lost his regalia in the disaster of the Wash, since only the baggage train foundered. With the Plantagenets, marvelous swords bearing legendary names appear in the regalia—the Sword of Smith Welland, the Sword of Tristram, and Curtein, the name of the broken sword that belonged to Ogier the Dane, one of Charlemagne's twelve peers.

Henry V pawned a crown to the mayor of Norwich for £800, wore a splendid crown to the battle of Agincourt and lost a piece of it to the Duke of Alençon's battle-axe, and two *fleurons* to a French esquire. Henry VIII, who had a marked weakness for stupendous collars of balas rubies, made a splash as a royal jewel collector and started negotiating for a jeweled pendant called The Three Brethren, which was looted from the tent of Charles the Bold, Duke of Burgundy, in 1475. Poor Mary Tudor, who won small happiness from her marriage to Philip II of Spain, at least secured a cheering wedding present in the form of La Peregrina, a pearl with one of the strangest histories of all famous jewels. It was found in the Pearl Islands off Panama by a Negro slave who won his freedom with it. After Mary's death it returned to Spain and was worn by Spanish queens on State occasions. When Philip V visited Versailles, Saint-Simon wrote, "I saw and handled at my ease the famous Peregrina that the King of Spain had that evening on the fold of his hat, hanging from a beautiful clasp of diamonds . . . it is perfectly shaped and bell-mouthed like those little pearls which are musk scented."

Joseph Bonaparte sensibly took La Peregrina away with him when he abdicated in 1813. It was later inherited by Prince Louis Napoleon who, running seriously short of funds, took it to the Marquis of Abercorn to beg the name of a jeweler who might be prepared to buy it. In total silence the Marquis drew a check, handed it over, and that afternoon gave the pearl to his wife. From then on the poor lady was in constant anxiety since the pearl had never been bored and was so heavy it was always toppling out of its setting—once into the folds of a velvet train at Buckingham Palace, again into the upholstery of a sofa at Wind-

BILDARCHIV FOTO MARBURG

Crown, crown, who's got the crown?

Of all the royal headgear in Lord Twining's *A History of the Crown Jewels of Europe,* no piece is more renowned than the Hungarian Crown of Saint Stephen (above), and none has a like history of falling into the oddest hands and disappearing. Fought over during ten centuries as the symbol of Hungary's turbulent kingship and nationhood, it has on occasion been hidden in a cushion by a lady-in-waiting, concealed in the disguise of a baby's bowl by a queen, buried in a swamp by revolutionary patriots, seized by Red chieftains—and now, strangest of all, it rests somewhere in the recesses not of the Hungarian but of the United States government, which will not say how it got it, where it is keeping it, who is in charge of it, and what we intend to do with it.

A low-slung cloth cap braced with gold ribs and ornamented with rough-cut stones and Byzantine enamel inlays, the crown is not a major jewelers' item as crowns go; yet a particular aura of mystery and mystique surrounds it. Pope Sylvester II appears to have sent at least part of it for the crowning and anointment of Hungary's first king, Stephen, in the year 1000; where the rest came from is still being debated. No one is sure whether its tilted cross was the result of design or accident. What is known is that for centuries, in order to get yourself made king of Hungary, you first had to gain possession of it by one means or another, which lent to the holder of the "Holy Crown" far greater powers than those of dynastic birth.

The Hapsburgs commandeered it; Kossuth's patriots and Bela Kun's Communists in turn seized it from them; now America has it, and this would be enough to make John F. Kennedy Hungary's rightful king.

How did we get it? The State Department will say only that it was "conveyed voluntarily" into American "custody" near the end of World War II. Press dispatches of the time, though, reported that American armed forces intercepted it on its journey from Hungary to Swiss refuge. On what basis are we holding it? To an inquiry from HORIZON the State Department replies, "In trust by US authorities as property of the Hungarian nation." By which authorities? No reply. Where? Cannot be divulged. Can it be seen and photographed? Absolutely *not*. If it is "property of the Hungarian nation," why don't we return it? Reply: Because it is property of a "special status . . . not eligible for restitution under clauses . . . of the Peace Treaty." What "special status" and why not eligible for restitution since, as the Department tells us, the crown has "profound historical and symbolic importance . . . to the Hungarian people"? Reply: "The Department does not regard it . . . opportune . . . to enter into public discussion of this or other sensitive aspects of the situation. . . ."

Which means, in lay English, Please shut up and go away, and it leaves, among other questions, the uneasy suspicion that the Department may simply have mislaid or lost it.

sor Castle. La Peregrina, bored at last and infinitely safer, is now owned by the present Duke of Abercorn.

Beautiful and coveted jewels with superb names crowd Lord Twining's book—the Sancy, the Mirror of Portugal, the Côte de Bretagne, the Orloff Diamond (once the stolen eye of a Buddha), the Blue Diamond, the Azra, and the Moon of the Mountains. What is astonishing is that so many of Europe's crown jewels have survived. The French collection, for obvious reasons, suffered punishing losses, and two major sales—that of the French Crown Jewels in 1887 and the auction of Russian State Jewels at Christie's in 1927—dispersed these astounding collections (Lord Twining provides both catalogues, with a great many illustrations). The Polish regalia was destroyed by the Prussians; the reliquary Crown of Saint Louis miraculously escaped a direct hit during the bombing of Dresden; and perhaps the most memorable escape story of all is the one of the Hanoverian crown jewels that were hidden at dead of night from the Prussians, buried in royal tombs (though out of respect they had not the nerve to disturb the ashes of the Electress Sophia), and later shipped to England. The late Queen Mary recalled having been told by her aunt, the Grand Duchess of Mecklenburg-Strelitz, of an encounter at Calais with a Hanoverian lady who "asked whether the Grand Duchess would give her a passage to England because she had the Hanoverian crown jewels sewn into her dress and that the crown was inside her hat . . . of course the Grand Duchess consented readily." In belated retribution Kaiser Wilhelm II's personal crown was almost burgled from Schloss Hohenzollern in 1954, but the burglar at the last moment suffered a pang of awe and made off with some snuffboxes instead.

Just occasionally you catch a quick, vivid glimpse of some of the women who wore the jewels and clearly had a personal feeling for them—Queen Louise of Prussia, saying about her pearls, with a pretty sorrow, "I loved them very much and kept them back when I had to give up my diamonds. They were better suited to me for they signified tears, and I have shed so many"; Marie Antoinette, who preferred light settings, constantly changing the settings of her own selection of crown jewels, turning them into gay little wreaths and knots and pompons, and wearing, with a negligent disrespect, the Regent, Sancy, and Mazarin diamonds on an aigrette of heron's feathers, or as drops of water on garlands of flowers.

Besides its obvious value to historians and those with a professional interest in the subject, the book is a wonderfully rich plum pudding, a dipping-book, full of great crowns that accompanied coronation and death, side by side with the incomparable trivia, the buttons and bows, done in priceless stones, of history; full of death, violence, fear, holy relics, debt, reverence, superstition, avarice, frivolity, pomp, innumerable swords, which may or may not have belonged to Charlemagne (whose teeth were presented to the Cathedral of Aix in 1349), and ravishing Golden Fleeces in brilliants, rubies, cat's-eyes, emeralds, opals, garnets, topazes, and hyacinths, each with its odd little sheep slung in a rather sad huddle from the pendant base.

Here, even though obliquely, is something of European eco-nomic, social, and constitutional history. The briefest glance at the Russian collection, with its implacable wealth, its exquisitely controlled and often simple design, and its deep understanding of jewels and their setting, makes the Revolution a perfectly logical conclusion to the chapter. Most of these jewels have witnessed important, if not always great events. Some of them, one hopes, have even gained a little gentleness and human affection in their royal progress.

During his long research Lord Twining's lumber-room complex has been rewarded several times: he has unearthed a Polish ivory sceptre in a secondhand bookshop in Belgrade, crowns in a cupboard in a Berlin museum, and tiaras in a Vatican attic. Indefatigable still, he has plans for a second volume, which may be called *European Regalia*. His intention is that it should be a series of essays outlining the origin, historical development, and use of royal ornaments, together with some examination of the philosophical ideas behind their existence. Some six chapters are already drafted, and Lord Twining is at present thinking over the possibility of publishing Part II in several self-contained volumes. This new enterprise "has to take a back seat as a spare-time job," as its author, though officially retired, is still fully committed. He is on the boards of a bank, a finance house, and a trading company, all of them interested in the development of East Africa. During the six or seven months of the year that he spends in England (for the rest he is in his house in Kenya), he attends the House of Lords "as often as I can make my contribution, especially on African affairs." He is chairman of numerous boards, foundations, and institutes with interests in African affairs. Lady Twining, a doctor, is actively engaged in Red Cross and public health work both in Kenya and England. The second volume must wait its turn.

During the last two years of Lord Twining's governorship of Tanganyika, when African nationalism was well on its way, he says he sometimes thought a good subtitle for his *History of the Crown Jewels of Europe* might be *The Story of European Nationalism*. Looking at Catherine II's staggeringly opulent and beautiful Imperial Crown of Russia, with its two climbing rows of giant pearls, its thick frost of diamonds, and its triumphant topmost spinel, one suddenly thinks of Alice, who reached the Eighth Square, found that a golden crown had materialized on her head as promised, and then "got up and walked about—rather stiffly just at first, as she was afraid that the crown might come off." Golden and heavy, iced with jewels as recklessly as overambitious birthday cakes, sacred but surely none too comfortable to wear, the crowns eventually fell off all over Europe, no matter how stiffly their regular royal owners walked about. It's good to have them—old, legendary, beautiful, slightly operatic, and now perfectly harmless—preserved inside book covers.

Siriol Hugh-Jones is an English journalist and critic who has contributed to Punch, *the* Tatler, *and other periodicals. She has also been an editor of* Vogue *and has broadcast for the BBC.*

Their Majesties' Splendor

A Portfolio of Crowns

Headpiece of a Humbled Emperor

When he died in 1106, the Holy Roman Emperor, Henry IV of Germany, was under a ban of excommunication. For a time it had been waived, when he made his famous pilgrimage to Canossa, and waited three days in the snow (according to legend) before receiving absolution from Pope Gregory VII. But only in 1111 was the sentence finally lifted, and the Emperor properly interred in the cathedral at Speyer. When his body was removed to a new mausoleum in 1900, many royal ornaments were found, among them his burial crown, made of gilded copper, with four fleurs-de-lis and a single arch. Inside the crown was a silk bonnet embellished with gold embroidery.

Princess Blanca's Dowry

Princess Blanca, the daughter of Henry IV of England, brought the crown which is named for her to Heidelberg in 1402 for her marriage to Ludwig III, the Elector Palatine. Already it was ancient; an English inventory of 1399 refers to this delicate tracery circle of twelve gem-set gold roses and lilies as "old jewelry." Actually no one knows whether the crown is of English, French, or other origin; it has been called the Bohemian Crown, apparently on the grounds that it was either once taken to Bohemia, or came to England with Anne of Bohemia, the daughter of Charles IV and the consort of Richard II.

"Dei Gratia...Imperator"

Sometimes called the Crown of Charlemagne, or the Nuremberg Crown, this dazzling octagon of gold plates, variously enameled and encrusted with precious stones, was for centuries the supreme emblem of the sovereign who bore the title of Holy Roman Emperor. It seems to have been made at a monastery on Lake Constance for the Emperor Otto I in about 961, and possession of it later became a highly important asset for claimants to the throne. On the panels are depicted scenes from the Old Testament, the one visible being the Lord enthroned between two angels, under the inscription: PER ME REGES REGNANT.

Tower Treasure

Perhaps the most famous of all crown jewels are those guarded by the red-coated warders of the Tower of London, among them the crown, orb, rod, and sceptre first used at the coronation of Charles II in 1661 (and refurbished by later sovereigns). Mounted on the sceptre (right center) is the largest brilliant known, the First Star of Africa, cut from the Cullinan diamond, which was given to Edward VII by the Transvaal.

The crown takes the name Saint Edward's from an ancient crown that was destroyed under Cromwell and may have been Edward the Confessor's. The orb is made of pure gold ("It is very heavy," said Queen Victoria, when told she should carry it). It was involved in the notorious attempt to steal the regalia in 1671 by an Irishman named Colonel Blood. King Charles, admiring Blood's audacity, pardoned and pensioned him.

The Duke's Fur Cap

"Cozy crowns for cold-weather kings" the author of the preceding article, Siriol Hugh-Jones, calls the Russian crowns bordered in sable fur that are now in the Kremlin Museum. The oldest of them is known as Monomakh's Cap, after Vladimir Monomakh, duke of Kiev in the twelfth century. In an effort to support their claim to divine sanction, Russian rulers encouraged a tradition that this cap was a gift of the Byzantine emperor to Saint Vladimir in 988, but the modern view gives it a much later date. We know for certain only that it was used as a coronation crown by Ivan IV in 1547.

English Luster on King Louis's Head

One of the most splendid crowns known to history was made in 1722 for the coronation of Louis XV of France. Of the dozens of diamonds ornamenting it, two are exceptionally large and perfect—the Regent, in the fleur-de-lis at the front of the crown; and the Sancy, at the very top. The Sancy had belonged to Charles I of England, and was given up only in payment of his Queen's debts. During the Revolution the Regent was stolen, recovered, pawned to raise money, and then fixed to the hilt of Napoleon's sword. The crown itself, which is displayed in the Louvre, is now set with paste imitations.

A Crown that Escaped the Moors

Invading Spain in the eighth century, the Moors were astounded at the wealth of the Visigothic kingdoms there, and acquired much of it—including their crowns. But a few were secreted away and survived intact, such as this one, a votive crown made for Recevinthus, a Visigoth who ruled from 653 to 672. It was brought out from hiding when a Toledo peasant stumbled upon an ancient cache in 1858. Votive crowns were gifts by kings to be hung above an altar and not necessarily worn. This one is in the form of a jeweled circlet from the lower rim of which hang letters set with garnets and colored glass, reading RECCESVINTHUS REX OFFERET.

ON THE HORIZON

DRAWINGS BY NICHOLAS SOLOVIOFF

The Baron Haussmann, as Wolf Von Eckardt observes ("The Man Who 'Destroyed' Paris," page 50), was undoubtedly the Robert Moses of his time; whether Moses is the Haussmann of *his* time is a question less easy to answer. Von Eckardt is in general sympathetic to Moses, though between the lines of his references one can read an awareness that sympathy for New York's Grand Panjandrum of the parks and parkways is a minority view. Even the news that Moses had recently put aside the mantle of some five of his seven high offices did not soften the hearts of those who see in him a dedicated enemy of New York City and what little remains to make it livable.

But the Commissioner (he must still be commissioner of *something*) is a redoubtable fellow, and the track of his progress across the years is littered with the whitened bones of people who underestimated him. This editor can claim to have made such a mistake only in a modest way, in the pages of HORIZON ("A Memorandum: From Julius Caesar to Robert Moses," March, 1959), when commending to him Caesar's example in banning wheeled vehicles from the center of Rome. I thought I had found a canny device to needle him, but shortly there arrived a gracious letter from the Moses *Hauptquartier* in Babylon, complimenting me on the piece and adding: "By way of evidence that the Roman experience was not entirely new to me, I attach a copy of a talk I gave in Philadelphia several years ago." There was the whole thing—dated 1946.

The only groups in New York who have successfully opposed Moses are West Side housewives and Greenwich Village beatniks. When he tried to convert a Central Park playground into a parking lot, marching down on it with bulldozers and a squad of police, mothers with massed baby carriages stopped him. When he tried to push a four-lane highway through Washington Square, the enlightened if slightly odd-ball forces of downtown bourgeois Bohemia —with a discreet and still mysterious assist from Tammany Hall—blocked him again. Moses favors the automobile. Whether New York is to be made livable for automobiles or for people is what the arguments over Moses are all about.

Moses has opened New York up to the automobile in somewhat the same way that Haussmann, with his boulevards, opened up Paris. So doing, Haussmann made Paris into the supreme city of the sidewalks, an unsurpassed playground for the pedestrian, with its sense of life both immediate and in the large, its long vistas and close-in cafés. Moses with his parkways, on the other hand, has made New York into a magnificent city to enter or leave, but at the price of strangling it at the center. From his sweeping curves of concrete the dazzled motorist is greeted with an unsurpassed and constantly shifting panorama of Manhattan's bridges and towers, only to be dumped unceremoniously into the cramped and crazy chaos of its auto-infested streets. Haussmann is well-remembered with good reason; Moses's fate may not be so lucky.   E. L.

THEATRE

By ROBERT HATCH

Melodrama on Broadway: Our Secret Lives Are Showing

Grammarians of the theatre distinguish four principal dramatic modes: tragedy, comedy, melodrama, and farce. Another way to handle this structural pedantry is to borrow a word from antique physiology and define these terms as the humors of the theatre. For just as the learned doctors could scarcely expect to find a man who was totally choleric or utterly phlegmatic, so it is almost impossible to cite a play that is, say, tragedy pure and simple.

An exception may be that nerve-shattering machine of careening ice floes, blazing orphanages, screaming buzz-saws and virgins outscreaming them which, from about 1850 to World War I, set the tone and made the money in the commercial theatre. This was melodrama, 200 proof. But it was so because it was a synthetic concoction, made by abstracting from drama an element that had existed there long before the word melodrama was coined. It is as though a culinary sensationalist, knowing that garlic is the most arresting ingredient in a salad, were to present his diners with a garlic salad. Such a dish would predictably dominate the meal, as indeed melodrama for a time dominated the theatre. But it would likely give garlic a bad name, as those plays have turned melodrama into a term of abuse. We pretend to be offended by the taste of it, whereas in fact our theatre would be pale and insipid without it.

Just what is it that we are talking about? Unfortunately it is easier to assume that everyone understands what melodrama is than to define the term. Stark Young, coping with the problem in that superb breviary, *The Theater*, says: "One of the traits of farce and melodrama . . . is exaggeration. . . . Their flight is reckless, they are the playwright's trip to the moon. . . . Melodrama is free to avoid the tragic finality, to evade its conclusion. . . . Both farce and melodrama take the cash and let the credit go; they eat their cake and have it too." That says something about how melodrama functions; it certainly suggests why it invigorates the stage and the audience. Eric Bentley, writing a few years ago in *The New Republic*, may have come closer to a definition with: "If art imitates life, it should be added

that while naturalistic art imitates the surfaces, 'melodramatic' art imitates what is beneath the surface. It is a matter, then, of finding external representation—symbol—for what cannot be photographed or described." And that ties in with a remark by M. Willson Disher (in *Melodrama*) that "insensibility to the absurd" is always a hallmark of melodrama. What goes on beneath the surface, the Freudian motion, is indeed absurd; and it is no coincidence, I think, that the reek of melodrama is particularly strong in the playhouses during this era of the Theatre of the Absurd. Melodrama does not prevail merely because it keeps us on the edge of our seats; by its use the fires that rage in our bosoms, the rats that gnaw at our brains, are brought on stage to be faced and, just possibly, faced down. Which foregoing will have to serve as a definition.

In view of all this it may be entertaining to trace the vein of melodrama in the current season. And that may serve the purpose of stopping people from crying out, as though they had discovered a toad in their bath, every time someone on stage does something or says something that the observer would not attempt in his wildest moments (however often he may have cherished the thought of it in his secret reveries).

Calculated Risk by Joseph Hayes, whose *The Desperate Hours* was an almost inexhaustible success as novel, play, and movie, is a good point of departure because it is a melodrama in the old gaslight sense, and we no longer see many of them. It lacks any of those climaxes of fire or flood that punctuated the most ambitious of the earlier thrillers (an airplane does roar in through a fearful fog, but the runway is off stage). However, the villain is a creature so besotted by greed and hate that he trembles and jerks and suffers a repertory of disfiguring tics. The plot is a variation on the widow's foreclosed mortgage. In this case a splendid old New England woolen mill, an enterprise dignified by the highest craftsmanship and the warmest paternalism, is threatened with worse than death by a raid on its common stock. The day is saved by the profligate elder son (played by Joseph Cotten), who in the hour of crisis is able to meet the scornful eyes of his dead father (a bust is provided for the purpose) and who shows an unsuspected, but apparently inherited, capacity for board-room trickery in a righteous cause. The play balances on the situation made immortal generations ago in the line, "There is a traitor in our midst," and all in all I spent an excellent evening. I suspect, however, that nostalgia gripped me as powerfully as the proceedings on stage. Thirty years ago Grey's Drug Store, that lodestone for stage-struck youths, could supply cut-rate seats for a show like this almost any night in the week.

At the other end of the scale is Harold Pinter's *The Dumbwaiter,* which has been offered this season in a double bill with his *The Collection.* This is anti-drama, Theatre of the Absurd, or whatever term you apply to the play whose main theme, whose central character, you might say, is its unspoken implication. The situation in *The Dumbwaiter* is certainly melodramatic: two gunmen, Ben and Gus, are waiting in a basement room for someone unknown to them who will presently come through the door and whom they will kill according to orders. They are great men for orders, these two; and the play turns to farce when the dumb-waiter in a building they had thought untenanted springs into action and sends down a succession of peremptory chits for dishes so numerous and varied that one must envision a bustling restaurant on the floor above. The two make hysterical, hopeless efforts to comply with an authority that is manifestly irrational—authority is their religion, and reason is not at issue.

The play bristles with melodramatic detail—the tense waiting, the quick flares of rage, the shocking eruption of the dumb-waiter (I was reminded of secret passages and bodies in closets), the book of matches slipped quietly under the door, and the empty corridor when the door is snatched open. Gus and Ben are two more men in thrall to Godot; like all true believers, what they expect for their devotion is justice ("Why did he send us matches if he knew there was no gas?"). The horror for them is that theirs turns out to be a personal Godot.

I won't stop over *The Collection.* It is a drawing-room comedy, with the difference that of the three men in the cast (there is also a woman) two are homosexual and one is ambiguous. This makes room for lively permutations, and the proceedings are witty at the expense of our skin-deep conventions; but the extravagance of the conflicts and alliances is more ironic than melodramatic.

José Quintero has revived O'Neill's *Desire Under the Elms* at Circle in the Square. It is a play animated by melodrama as the Greeks knew it: a father and son mortally opposed, a mother destroying her child in a mad attempt to end the struggle. Whenever *Desire Under the Elms* is revived (and it happens frequently), it is like a gale sweeping the contemporary stage clean of trivialities

and the fine shavings of sentiment. Still, I think it is a case where melodrama may be used as a term of criticism. O'Neill rouses pity and terror with his melodrama, but he cannot sublimate them in his tragedy, for it lacks the stature that would allow an audience to find its own significance in a universal design. Tragedy is no longer held to be the exclusive realm of gods and kings, but to quote Stark Young again, in a paraphrase of the standard definitions: the tragic in drama is "the struggle of the individual will against eternal law, the struggle of the good with the good." Old Ephraim Cabot seems to be generating his own law; it is not an inescapable one that tempers us all. And Eben, his son, and Abbie, the wife of one and stepmother of the other, lack the virtue that might give their fate the permanence and breadth of legend. A tragedy that does not rise to inevitability subsides into morbidity.

This latest production was built upon the extraordinary energy and projective powers of George C. Scott, Colleen Dewhurst, and Rip Torn. It was a muscular and compelling presentation, but I felt it did not compose into a unified work. The solo resourcefulness of the actors may have been too pressing for Quintero to harness in the time available. More likely, theatre-in-the-almost-round works to the serious disadvantage of a play set on three nearly equal and mutually antagonistic points. A centrifugal motion is almost unavoidable, with the actors hurling themselves at the audience instead of at one another.

*W*hat everyone noted about Peter Feibleman's *Tiger, Tiger, Burning Bright* is that at last we are shown a play about Negroes which is not about the Negro problem. But I don't think anyone has made the related point that it is not about the Negro question only because, with one inconsequential exception, there are no white people in it. It is not yet possible to mix the races on stage (or for that matter in fiction) without race becoming an element in the plot. This is a reflection, surely, but it is a reflection on society, not on the theatre. Color still makes a point that is additional to whatever point the playwright is concerned about, and as long as that is true Negro actors, however accomplished, will find the great majority of central roles closed to them. That it will not always be true can be predicted from the increasing frequency with which Negroes appear on stage (and in the movies) in situations where color is irrelevant. I don't mean the traditional parts of domestics and raffish hangers-on; there is a wide area of supporting roles in which the color of an actor's skin now sets off no response. An interracial *Romeo and Juliet* or *Doll's House* may someday be a matter of no special comment, but in this area the theatre will follow the mores, not create them.

Meanwhile one can judge from the performance of *Tiger, Tiger* how much the barrier of racial awareness is costing us in stage talent. Few productions display such a consistently high level of individual craft or so unified an embodiment of the author's intent and the director's interpretation (the director here was Joshua Logan). The leads were Claudia McNeil, Alvin Ailey, and Diana Sands, but the rest of the company moved around and through their focal struggle with a grace and power for which the conventional word "supporting" is inadequate.

In terms of melodrama the play intensified, and provided overt symbols for, a familiar enough experience—the masks of accommodation we wear to make personal relations tolerable. It is melodrama, not realism, because it transforms proclivities into deeds and inadequacies into vices. Factually, the house of illusion constructed by Feibleman could never have stood; symbolically, though, such houses stand on every street. In more specific terms the play offered a series of tableaux in high melodrama: the noble son exposed as a thief, the prim maiden discovered in her whore's raiment, the dream of honor on which the mother has built her matriarchy shattered by a word. But the melodrama here is also in the service of tragedy, for good does struggle with good, and the fate of the family is not irrelevant to our general condition.

Whatever swamps and miasmas Tennessee Williams may still have in store for us, his tone from *Period of Adjustment,* through *The Night of the Iguana,* to *The Milk Train Doesn't Stop Here Anymore* has been relatively free of horrors. By comparison with the past, the mood of these plays is almost benign.

In *The Milk Train* he essays the device, technically interesting and theatrically exciting, of presenting a conventionally tragic situation in the vocabulary of comedy. The tension thus built can, I think, be called melodrama; to laugh in the teeth of death is surely a melodramatic, not to say heroic, extravagance. I understand that Ionesco develops a variation of the same theme in a recent play, *Le Roi Se Meurt (The King Expires).*

Like Belle Poitrine of *Little Me,* Flora Goforth in *The Milk Train* has risen from dubious obscurity to wealth and social power by a lively and judicious commerce in husbands. Also like Patrick Dennis's heroine, she is now writing her memoirs and for that purpose has installed in her complex of Italian coastal villas a battery of tape recorders and an intercom system that gives her instant command of her secretary at any hour of the day or (more frequently) night. But unlike Belle, Flora Goforth is dying, dying most painfully and in full knowledge of the nearness of the hour. Flora is a clown, and she is dying to an accompaniment of bells and slapstick; nevertheless, there is the fact of it.

She has planned to spend her last summer in virtual retirement, repaying herself for the loss of society by tormenting her secretary, a Vassar girl with a bun, who is a particularly suitable target in that she is mourning her late husband. Mourners are Flora's natural victims, the more so since she foresees that she will have none.

This routine of dictation and rabbit-punching is upset by the unannounced arrival of a young man clad in *lederhosen,* wearing a knapsack and holding a somewhat scuffed volume of his poetry in his hand. As Flora soon learns from her sharp-taloned chum Signora Condotti (formerly Mrs. Ridgeway), this Chris Flanders, an itinerant constructor of mobiles, has been present at the demise of so many rich and lonely ladies that he is known the length of the French and Italian coast as the Angel of Death. This does not much daunt Flora, who is aware in any case that her course is run, but she is determined not to be duped. She will take on Chris as an ultimate lover, but for free-loaders bent on exchanging spirituality for room and board, the milk train no longer stops at Casa Goforth.

As long as Williams keeps to the purgative exchanges between a pair of dragons too old to bother with hypocrisy, as long as he shocks us out of complacency toward such matters as individual morality and universal mortality, he is pertinent and very funny. And since Hermione Baddeley and Mildred Dunnock were handling his foils, the stage sparkled like a bowl of rhinestones.

Chris, the transcendental beach boy, is a more uneasy element. He could be as bitingly droll as the two harridans, with their costume wigs and cosmetic smattering of Italian, but it is not clear that the author intends Angel of Death as an entirely ironic nickname. Paul Roebling played the role as hygienically as a young man can when he must expose to maximum view a pair of legs that are a little too shapely and a little too evenly tanned to elicit the unreserved admiration of the males in the audience. But he was made to say some very silly things in the manner of Eastern mysticism, and I got the strong impression that he was about to bestow apotheosis on Flora Goforth when the final curtain cut off my view. If so, this is carrying melodrama to the point of blasphemy—by which I mean an offense against the God-given sanity of the audience. It is enough that Williams should make us feel for Flora: when he implies that her death will be an assumption (and what else is that mobile, glittering in the light of the last scene, meant to imply?), he falls into bathos. For Flora has great relevance as a bitch and none at all as a saint. But whatever its deficiences as philosophic tragedy, *The Milk Train* was a theatrical evening of wit and pertinent exaggeration.

Melodrama, then, abides; it can be found in almost any play that cuts beneath our skin. It is the embodiment in action of what we know our secret lives to be. For the secret life is not so much a self-delusion as evidence that few people can make art of their personal histories. Melodrama is the armature that a man would need to give his days and years some communicable shape—and that, finally, will have to rest as the definition.

Liszt and Chopin: Appassionato, Diminuendo, Morendo

Musicians do not often write well about music. Their own language is so rich that they do not feel happy using ours. True, Richard Wagner issued a number of thundering manifestoes in C major, and Berlioz poured out some of his extra energy in extravagant prose, but they are difficult to read today; while the columns that Debussy wrote (and signed "M. Croche") are unexpectedly acid, though not unexpectedly witty. In the anthology *Composers on Music,* edited by Sam Morgenstern and published in 1956 by Pantheon, there are relatively few pages that can be read without rueful amusement or sympathetic distress.

A composer very seldom writes about other composers. His own mission fills his mind. How can he estimate another man's success when he is trying to build his own? How can he give ear to a stranger's message before he has uttered his own gospel? Sometimes, though, a composer will show his understanding of a colleague's work by performing it as a soloist, or by conducting it in an orchestral presentation, or, as a particularly graceful compliment, by writing a series of variations upon one of its themes. Thus, Rachmaninoff, a rather forbidding introvert, gave a number of Scriabin recitals to help the widow after Scriabin's early death, and honored Kreisler with elegant transcriptions of *Liebesleid* and *Liebesfreud.*

For all his brilliance and for all his exhibitionism, Franz Liszt was unexpectedly and charmingly modest when he dealt with other musicians. He was himself a remarkable composer. His most distinguished pieces survive with almost undiminished vitality; the form which he virtually invented, the symphonic poem, was a profound stimulus to his successors; and in his later work there are astonishing anticipations of modern experiments in tonality. Yet he was phenomenally generous in acknowledging the achievements of other music makers—Bellini, Berlioz, Schumann, Schubert, Wagner, Borodin, and above all, Chopin.

Chopin and Liszt: they are a special case of that curiously paired phenomenon which appears sometimes in literature, often in painting and music. First comes a creator, and then a younger rival who starts by emulating

and adapting, and at last stands out as a creator on almost the same level. In recent times we have seen at least three such pairs: Wagner and Sibelius, Debussy and Ravel, Stravinsky and Prokofiev. (Think, for instance, of the musical versions of the Nibelung and the Kalevala legends, even of *Siegfried's Rhine Journey* and *Lemminkaïnen's Homeward Journey;* of *Children's Corner* and *Mother Goose, Saraband* and *Pavane;* of *Petrouchka* and *Chout, Rite of Spring* and *Scythians.*) But seldom has the pair been so close and sympathetic as Chopin and Liszt. Liszt constantly expressed the warmest and most sincere admiration for Chopin, reviewing his concerts, performing his works, writing transcriptions of his songs, and carrying forward his musical ideas; while Chopin said he wished he could "steal" Liszt's art of playing his *Etudes.*

Liszt is one of the few creative musicians who has ever written a book about another. In 1852, three years after Chopin's death, he published a biographical sketch of his friend. English translations came out here and in Britain, but have long been forgotten. Now, much overdue, a readable English version, translated by Edward N. Waters and titled *Frederic Chopin by Franz Liszt,* is to be published here by The Free Press of Glencoe.

*T*his is not, however, a typical biography. Those who go to it for schematic facts and systematic judgments will be infuriated. It is a Rhapsody on the Theme of Chopin. Such a rhapsody, written by Liszt for piano and orchestra, would surely have been a masterpiece; indeed, I have often thought that his *Funérailles,* usually supposed to be a requiem for the victims of the 1848 Hungarian rebellion, contains some of his grief for the loss of his Polish friend. This, however, is in poetic prose, and it is not all by Liszt. Always generous in accepting collaboration, and always amorous, he evidently allowed some of it to be written or suggested by his mistress, Princess Carolyne of Sayn-Wittgenstein, a Polish lady of exuberant temper and passionate patriotism. To her, or to her influence over him, we owe long passages of wild and whirling words, like this description of George Sand listening to Chopin:

She brought to her listening the full power of her ardent genius, which had the rare quality, reserved only for a few elect, of perceiving beauty in any form of art and nature, a quality that might be that *second sight,* the superior gifts of which all nations acknowledge in women who are inspired. An entranced stare enables their vision to penetrate the bark, the covering, the coarse wrapping of form and permits them to glimpse, in its invisible essence, the soul there incarnated, the ideal that the poet and artist have conjured up under the swirl of notes or layers of color, the folds of marble, the shaping of stone, or the mysterious rhythms of verse. It is a quality dimly apprehended by most; its supreme manifestation, [etc., etc.]

Yet even these outpourings do at least give us the mystical atmosphere in which Chopin and Liszt often wrote, and which they in some measure converted into music. And elsewhere in the biography, whether from the pen of Liszt or from his Polish lady, there are facts and descriptions of great interest. There is an evocation of a party where Chopin was host, and played his own music to Heine, Meyerbeer, Delacroix, and the great Polish poet Mickiewicz. (I have been reading Mickiewicz's epic *Pan Tadeusz* again, and find that, with this biographical sketch, it makes a superb commentary on much of Chopin's finest music.) There is an account of Chopin's training. His first teacher, Zywny, was a devout admirer of Bach—which helps to explain why Chopin published a book of twenty-four *Préludes* in all the major and minor keys, and why he often prepared for a recital by playing the *Well-tempered Clavier;* and it was Prince Anton Radziwill (whose family once owned 800,000 serfs and had jeweled harnesses for the horses) who paid for Chopin's entire education— through an intermediary, to spare him embarrassment. I have been playing Chopin for forty years now and, apart from technical problems, I have always found his polonaises and mazurkas by far the most difficult of his works, simply because I have never really seen the movements of these dances. The most consistently beautiful and original passage of this biography is a truly wonderful description of the polonaise, a magnificent procession danced through the great rooms, the galleries, and the gardens of a noble house, and of the mazurka, a gay flirtation combining hopeful challenge and melancholy renunciation, amorous simplicity with subtle paradoxical wit.

As it should, the book ends with a death scene. Like Keats and Hölderlin, Chopin was one of those artists who feel themselves inescapably destined for an early death. His faithful Scottish pupil, Jane Stirling, did nothing to delay it, by persuading him to visit her native land and play his music in the dank mists and dour streets of Glasgow and Edinburgh. The description of his last illness is touching and memorable. He expressly asked to be buried beside Bellini, and to have Mozart's *Requiem* sung at his funeral.

A sad life: romantic but without the strength for rapture; sensitive, but without the ruthlessness of Byron or the bravura of Berlioz. This book tells us much about Chopin, and treats him with the respect due a superb artist and a noble man. Yet (because its author was Magyar and his collaborator Polish) it plays down one aspect of his character and his art. Chopin wrote Polish music, but he also wrote French music. Sometimes his work has the nostalgic melancholy the Poles call *Zal,* and sometimes the swirling energy of the Slavic dances; but often it has the reticence of the well-bred Frenchman. His mother was Polish, but his father was French; he was born near Warsaw, but he died in Paris.

MOVIES

By HANS KONINGSBERGER

Love in Another Country (Where They Order it Better)

It must be twenty years ago that I saw the movie version of Fannie Hurst's *Back Street* with Charles Boyer and Margaret Sullavan, but there is one crucial scene in it which I remember vividly. Margaret Sullavan is riding in an open carriage on her way to the Mississippi riverboat where her fiancé is waiting for her. They will embark together and be married aboard. A former suitor, an unpleasant but hardly malicious character, happens to appear on the scene and delays her so long that she misses the boat. She misses that boat with utmost finality: her young man, thinking she has stood him up, sails without her and marries someone else. Eventually the two lovers meet again and the fantastic misunderstanding is cleared up, but it is too late. They spend the rest of their lives vainly trying to somehow mend their broken romance.

I hope I remember all this correctly; I never dared go see this film again—it impressed me so at an impressionable stage of life. (A new, 1961 movie of the same name is best forgotten.)

Back Street is a classic example of Love thwarted by Matter; of romance, that is, stopped in its tracks, not by lack of response or emotion in people, but by an ironically trivial stumbling block thrown in its path by blind fate. The device of the missed rendezvous (undelivered or intercepted letters, a telephone that stops ringing a second too soon, interrruptions of all sorts at critical moments, serve equally well) has always been popular with novelists as well as movie makers, but its tragic consequences in *Back Street* are most unusual for a Hollywood picture. The drama of life's timing in matters of love, the "lost chance," is rarely taken seriously in American movies, and for the good reason that American philosophy is against admitting the existence of such a thing as the lost chance.

*T*hink of any American movie in which love's consummation is prevented by the whims of time and space. Cannot fate be counted upon to present the couple in trouble with another chance, and yet another one? And even if it takes its own sweet time about it, won't the hero and heroine—be it five years later—appear as young, as eager, and as desiring? But not only is fate seldom persistently unfriendly, it is actually mankind's most dependable marriage counselor. For if two people are "meant for each other," they will have another chance, and if they are just mistakenly carried away by a feeling of the moment, fate can be depended on to throw enough obstacles in their path to give them time to come to their senses—or to enable Mr. or Miss Right to appear. When things go awry in love's obstacle course, it's only seemingly bad luck. In the end, all turns out to have been for the best in this best of all possible worlds. In the economics of love American movie makers have remained die-hard Adam Smith liberals.

The Continental tradition is quite different. In French movies the tragedy of timing spells a missed chance that rarely if ever is presented again. In *Sous les Toits de Paris* the cops prevent, in a classic movie tradition, love's bliss, and they do so forevermore. In *Les Enfants du Paradis* the obstacles really exist only in the mind of the overserious lover, but when he has surmounted them, it is too late anyway. In *The Cousins* a chance meeting of the girl with someone else not only ruins a beginning love but ends by destroying the young man's life. *Shoot the Piano-Player* allows a second chance (though years later, and with another woman), but that one too slips away when the hero hesitates one second too long. French motion pictures underline the ephemeral character of happiness in love. Fate

is whimsical and cruel, and when the rare right moment is not grabbed, it slips by irredeemably.

Compare two movies about married love; that is to say, married-to-someone-else love—*Brief Encounter* and *The Facts of Life. Brief Encounter,* of course, was British, which means not quite European, but it happened to be quite Continental in spirit. *Facts of Life* is about as American as possible. In both these dissimilar movies a middle-aged man and woman, married to others, are in love and reach a moment where they want to dismiss everything but the need to lie in each other's arms. In both films they create this chance for themselves but find circumstances frustrating it.

In the British movie the frustrated love spells tragedy, in the American movie, comedy—and comedy made the more pleasing by our knowledge that it is all for the best that the man and woman cannot have their way. These lovers are middle-aged, which adds a nostalgic note but does not change the typicality of the treatments. The setting for the consummation of the British illicit love is an apartment, a borrowed one. Trevor Howard and Celia Johnson are interrupted in their meeting there, and fate thus cruelly forces on them a time lag in which their resolve evaporates and their old doubts and pangs of conscience, raised again, cannot be assuaged a second time. Soon afterward they separate forever (in a famous railway station scene), not relieved at heart but bitterly aware of a happiness never tasted and now lost for eternity.

The parallel setting to the borrowed apartment is in *Facts of Life* that most American of all institutes, a motel. The lovers-to-be, Bob Hope and Lucille Ball, have finally managed to duck husband, wife, children, friends, and P.T.A. meetings; now the heroine lends fate a hand by demanding coffee. Mr. Hope obediently sets out in his car for a short-order counter, but by the time he has acquired his container of coffee, he finds himself unable to retrace the route to the motel. When, after miles and miles of endless Los Angeles streets and well-nigh identical motels, he finds the right address, but not Miss Ball, who has given him up and gone home, he seems relieved rather than frustrated at the chaste ending to his evening.

In *Facts of Life* the hero and heroine have another try at the fulfillment of their passion. Here the movie lost much of its appeal for me (I liked the self-irony of love lost amidst identical motels), but it remained as typical as ever as it resorted to Hollywood's basic repertory of petty obstacles of the leaking-bedroom-roof type to keep the lovers out of bed. The comedies of the thirties used those tricks more amusingly—Fred Astaire tap dancing over the bridal suite to keep his true love, Ginger, out of the arms of her ill-matched husband; but where they are supposed to imply that people wanting each other cannot make it if the setting is less than perfect, they seem silly rather than funny. But, either way, they demonstrate the American reluctance to take passion and to take private love (as distinguished from love in abstracto) quite seriously. In the movie *Lolita,* vaguely based on the novel, I felt that James Mason crying over his lost girl friend presented an instance of splendid acting and splendid movie writing; but I was aware that he made the audience extremely uncomfortable with his tears. Such emotions are rare in American movies (and novels) because they are rare in American society: here the lover's despair is not a subject of romance but of psychoanalysis.

In a movie love-world, where opportunity is unlimited, where love is frustrated only if it is for everyone's good, and where, moreover, there is always an attractive man or woman ready and waiting in the background to console the jilted lady or suitor, it is hard to dramatize the real despair of love or jealousy. In the United States, society is romantic but individuals are not. Thus the pursuit of love can have no tragic ending, for if people are meant for each other, society will in the end be on their side. If it is not, this only shows that the love was unsuitable in the first place, and that the hero will be much better off with his childhood sweetheart (who, once she takes off her glasses, is quite pretty anyway); or that the heroine was really already in love with the understanding detective, journalist, or poor but honest friend of the hero.

In the European, the Continental, tradition, the chips are stacked differently. True love is rare, and the relationships and marriages of society have little to do with it. People are romantic but society is not. Thus the European pursuit of love is a race against time and place, as desperate as the American pursuit of the bandit by the sheriff. Society is the enemy of true love, and only sheer luck, great courage, and magnificent horsemanship on the obstacle course of life, can bring the star-crossed lovers together. At this point, the girl will certainly not send her man out for coffee. She knows time is precious. Soon fate may knock on the door and interrupt their embrace.

Neither love nor motion pictures fit snugly into little boxes, and I do not feel smug about this distinction between an American and a European philosophy on the subject of Love vs. Daily Life. For one thing, both approaches sketched here have in common something traditional, old-fashioned, "square," or whatever it may be called: they both *care,* though about different things to be sure. There is a whole spate of recent European imports that do not belong in either category, but seem to combine the worst of both worlds. In these pictures, products of the New and not so new Waves, love's course is frequently blocked by chance; but whether it is or is not, found and fulfilled love brings as little happiness as lost love. As in American movies, passion is not a very serious matter; as in French movies, society is not to be taken seriously, but then neither is life itself. For here we have an (international) philosophy of our years, once rather sloppily labeled existentialist, and more simply summed up as "Who cares anyway?" Such a concept may make a splendid movie *(L'Avventura)* or a dreary one *(The Eclipse),* for an artist, of course, can make everything out of anything. But this school will never give us a romantic film, for however romance may be treated, it is never bored with itself.

CHANNELS

By STEPHEN WHITE

The Hershey Bar: Is Advertising Really Necessary?

Every now and then the advertising industry pauses to salute those of its customers who have been most assiduous in the matter of opening the sluice gates. Pride of place invariably goes to the General Motors Corporation, which spends about $140 million a year in advertising; Procter & Gamble is rarely more than a few million dollars behind. Presumably these figures are made public *pour encourager les autres,* since it may be taken for granted that any self-respecting corporation would like to grow up to be General Motors, or at the very worst Procter & Gamble.

But to derive full-bodied satisfaction from these figures it is necessary to probe more deeply, into the affairs of less robust industrial titans who are able to scrape up only a million here and a million there for purposes of cajoling the general public.

Consider, for example, the Alberto-Culver Company: it is engaged in the manufacture and distribution of various kinds of gurry, which the public is encouraged to rub into its hair. According to *Advertising Age* Alberto-Culver in 1961 invested some $14,500,000 in advertising, which no one will deny is a nice piece of change. To put this figure in perspective, it is just about the sum expended during the same period by United States Steel. But there is a profound difference between these two industrial behemoths. U. S. Steel, shrewdly pushing its cold-rolled tin plate and its I beams in appropriate media, managed to roll up a neat $3 billion and a little bit over in sales. Alberto-Culver, on the other hand, had to make do with a mere $25,344,867 in revenues. Granted, this is a whole lot of hair oil, but all the same it means that for every dollar that came into the counting house, 57.2 cents went back out to buy advertising.

This stimulates a healthy curiosity. Alberto-Culver products come in handy tubes or jars or bottles, all of which cost money; they are neatly wrapped and crated. It must cost money to sell them and deliver them, and I assume that Mr. Alberto and Mr. Culver take a well-earned buck or two off the top. This can't leave a great deal for the hair oil itself, and it makes one wonder what the customer with the unruly hair is really getting. Or to put it another way, can it be that he is merely rubbing advertising into his hair? This is an entirely appropriate use for most advertising, but I find it hard to believe that it really keeps the hair down; it makes mine rise.

This kind of thing always bothers me. I get the same feeling when I see charcoal for sale in the nearest supermarket, to enable the householder to mistreat steaks and chops at a cost of $2,000 a ton for fuel. I remember being told once by a friend in the food-processing dodge that his product—corn flakes or gelatin dessert or something—really didn't cost anything at all, unless you were willing to carry your calculations out to several decimal places. The paper it was wrapped in, on the other hand, was a significant item. And the advertising that was necessary if the public was to be cajoled into buying it—*that* cost money!

Mind you, it bothers me, but I can put up with it and I am not complaining. The $25,344,867 that Alberto-Culver amassed in sales during 1961 is all part of the Gross National Product, and we all know how important that is. A country's might and status and comfort are measured by its GNP, and unless our GNP continues to rise we shall lose the Cold War and sink into insignificance, like Lichtenstein. It is my earnest hope that Alberto-Culver trebles its advertising and doubles its sales annually from here to eternity, because I have no wish to become a second-class power, or worse.

If I am disturbed at all, it is about the companies that are clearly not pulling their weight. The Prudential Insurance Company, for example. In sales it is the third largest corporation on the *Ad Age* list, collecting more than $9 billion during 1961. But it advertises barely half as much as Alberto-Culver. By rights, Prudential should be spending $10 billion or $11 billion a year on advertising, and then it could double the price of insurance and add a

whopping $15 billion or so to the Gross National Product. It's all very well to put up tall buildings and low-cost housing, but if Prudential would tend to its affairs it could do some real good for the country.

In this connection we should all wish to welcome the Hershey Chocolate Corporation into the fold, although I may be doing so somewhat prematurely. Hershey does not appear anywhere on the *Ad Age* list. In fact, advertising men do not like to speak of the Hershey company and would prefer to believe that it does not really exist at all but is only a hockey team. For Hershey, be it known, is as irresponsible as a company can get. Hershey does not advertise at all.

*N*ow any ad man can tell you what this sort of thing leads to. If a company, and in particular a company engaged in production of a perfectly ordinary staple for the mass market, does not advertise, that company's petals must wither and that company's flower must die. This is a natural law, like Universal Gravitation and Motivational Research.

And yet, despite all this higher knowledge, Hershey keeps on making more chocolate bars and selling more chocolate bars than anyone else who tries. They come in a drab package, which has never, in my memory, been redesigned. Hershey blithely makes its chocolate, and lays it down on the candy counter, and people come and buy it. Then, when those people grow older and desert the candy counter, their kids come and buy it. This may be inexplicable, but there it is. The whole procedure sounds vaguely anti-American, or at least antisocial. But the company, perhaps out of sheer spite, has built a model town and endowed a boys' school and supports that hockey team, so it is difficult to launch a serious attack against it.

Anyway, it may no longer be necessary. The word is that Hershey has entered the Canadian market. Since it has never undertaken to sell chocolate bars in Canada, Hershey fears that Canadians will not come and buy them, for the only Canadians who know about Hershey are the ones who play on the hockey team, and they have to watch their weight. Hence, Hershey is thinking seriously of laying on an advertising agency and hitting the Canadians over the airwaves and elsewhere.

I would like to believe that it will end there, over the border. But advertising is a drug, and the man who is most sensitive to it is the ad man himself. Soon the agency will compose a jingle, or coin a slogan, or invent a grammatical monstrosity which will so catch the company's fancy that Hershey will be unable to forbear sharing it with the American trade. In no time at all Hershey will go by Alberto-Culver as if the hair-oil boys were standing still, and make its honorable way onto the list of most-honored advertisers. What this will do to the chocolate bar I do not know, but I suppose it isn't really important.

Can This Drug Enlarge Man's Mind? CONTINUED FROM PAGE 31

Many and many a dream is mere confusion,
a cobweb of no consequence at all.
Two Gates for ghostly dreams there are: one gateway
of honest horn, and one of ivory.
Issuing by the ivory gate are dreams
of glimmering illusion, fantasies,
but those that come through solid polished horn
may be borne out, if mortals only know them.
I doubt it came by horn, my fearful dream—
too good to be true, that, for my son and me.

What Penelope is saying is that there are two categories, or channels, of subconscious insight: one, coming in through the "Gate of Horn," of things that "may be borne out" (that is, having to do with events, both present and future, in our actual lives) and the other, through the "Gate of Ivory," of apparently the sheerest fantasy. And it is certainly recognized by all students of psychical research that there is a deep current of the mind which brings to the surface (sometimes by way of dreams, but not necessarily always) raw data—an incoherent babbling, irresponsible glossolalia, sufficiently confusing to justify the epithet "glimmering illusion, fantasies." Clues as to this second traffic, when they do appear, are ambiguous; symbols are so fractured that for a long while they are quite unrecognizable.

Here lies one reason why many decades of modern psychical research into this anomalous traffic have produced such baffling and frustrating results. Another is that whereas the flow running through Penelope's "Gate of Horn" is as constant and copious as the daily tides, the springs that feed the "Gate of Ivory" seem sporadic and indeed capricious. No wonder then that psychoanalysis, which confines itself to the masses of sea wrack brought up through the "Gate of Horn" and stranded on the beaches of our waking mind, attracts such an army of deep-sea psychobiologists, while those who wait by the other water gate have but a few minnows to show after nearly three generations of research.

Psychoanalysis is concerned mainly with man's conflicts between his sexual urges and the taboos imposed upon him by society, and with the effects of these conflicts on his everyday living. But the traffic we associate with the "Gate of Ivory" deals with data apparently belonging to those higher registers of the mind which very few researchers outside the psychical field have even noticed. It is true that mystics and saints have reported, time and again, "out-of-this-world," indescribable experiences that did change their lives and bring a "better order" in their living. But these experiences came as the result of many years of severe mental and physical discipline carried out within a doctrinal frame of reference, which often brought them to the brink of insanity. For many

the experience was only a brief flash. For some it came two or three times during a lifetime of discipline. For instance Plotinus, so his biographer and disciple Porphyry tells us, only three times in his long life of striving for it attained to "the state." But until now there has been no other way of opening up this other passage of perception, of keeping it open for any length of time, or of doing it at will. How is this free flow of findings to be obtained?

We now recognize that our minds have, as oculists say of our eyes, not one but a number of focal lengths. The aperture of our understanding alters, in the way that we alter the aperture of our telescopes and microscopes to bring objects into clear focus at specific ranges. But, though our minds do shift, though our range of perception will at times change gear, we cannot make that shift deliberately, consciously. Nor when it occurs can we hold on to it. And when the most common, as well as the most profound shift—that from waking to sleeping—takes place, we are not able to observe it as we experience it. This problem has teased psychologists for sixty years, and the greatest of them, William James, saw that if it was to be solved, the experimenter must use psychophysical means on himself. He tried nitrous oxide as a means of enlarging consciousness, only to find that at a certain point communication ceased, and he came back murmuring, "The Universe has no opposite." Then he tried peyotl, the button cactus that grows along the Rio Grande and is used in the religious rites of Indians in the Southwest as a sacrament lending lucidity—only to be daunted by the stumbling block of severe nausea.

Leave chemicals aside for the moment. There is an "other" state of mind, known to and described by poets as well as higher mathematicians and other scientific geniuses, in which a deeply "insightful" process can take place. The current president of India, the philosopher Dr. Sarvepalli Radhakrishnan, has termed this process "integral thought" as against "analytic thought"—the latter being the inductive procedure whereby through the patient gathering, analysis, and arranging of data there would at last emerge a general "law." "Integral thought" is the art of the sudden insight, the brilliant hypothesis, the truly "creative" leap. To have truly original thought the mind must throw off its critical guard, its filtering censor. It must put itself into a state of depersonalization; and from such histories as Jacques Hadamard's *The Psychology of Invention in the Mathematical Field* we know that the best researchers, when confronting problems and riddles that had defied all solution by ordinary methods, did employ their minds in an unusual way, did put themselves into a state of egoless "creativity" which permitted them to have insights so remarkable that by means of these they were able to make their greatest and most original discoveries.

Paracelsus found that there was a "ledge of the mind," free of all caution, to which wine could lift him; there, though unable to hold a pen, he could still dictate, until intoxication swept him into speechlessness. Descartes, sleeping on the floor with writing paper beside him, scrawled down the insights that flashed across his mind in a half-waking state, when the creative and critical levels of his brain were both working. Harvey, the discoverer of the circulation of the blood, told his biographer Aubrey that if he stayed in a disused coal shaft in total dark and silence, his uninterrupted mind would reach a span it could not encompass above ground, when trying to "think regardless of consequence" amid the wary, hostile medical world of his day. Henri Poincaré, the great French mathematician, described his subliminal processes of discovery in these words: "It is certain that the combinations which present themselves to the mind in a kind of sudden illumination after a somewhat prolonged period of unconscious work are generally useful and fruitful. . . . This, too, is most mysterious. How can we explain the fact that, of the thousand products of our unconscious activity, some are invited to cross the threshold, while others remain outside?" (In his classic study of poetic creation, *The Road to Xanadu*, John Livingston Lowes cited this passage as bearing on the deep movements of Coleridge's own psyche.)

Can LSD provide any assistance to the creative process? Even when given under the best of conditions, it may do no more (as Aristotle said when appraising and approving the great Greek Mysteries) than "give an experience." Thereafter the subject must himself work with this enlarged frame of reference, this creative *schema*. If he will not, the experience remains a beautiful anomaly, a gradually fading wonder—fading because it has no relevance to "the life of quiet desperation" which Thoreau saw most of us living and which we cannot help but live.

What, then, should be done about it? LSD is certainly one of the least toxic chemicals man has ever put inside his system. Compared with alcohol, nicotine, coffee—our three great stand-bys—it could be called almost a docile mare as against these mettlesome stallions, so far as most people are concerned. Is it of any use with psychotics? Most researchers doubt it. With the extreme neurotic? Again there seems to be considerable question. Although among these categories LSD appears to do no physical harm, cases of severe adverse psychological effects have been reported. It is the unique quality of *attention* which LSD can bestow that will or will not be of benefit. Intensity of attention is what all talented

people must obtain or command if they are to exercise their talent. Absolute attention—as we know from, for example, Isaac Newton's and Johann Sebastian Bach's descriptions of the state of mind in which they worked—is the most evident mark of genius functioning. On the other hand, the masterful Sigmund Freud remarked that psychoanalysis, even when exercised by himself, would not work with the extreme neurotic because of the hypertrophied ego-attention which such a patient had sacrificed his life to build up. The psychotic is even more absorbed in his distortive, self-obsessed notion of reality. Give, then, either of these victims of their own egos still greater capacity to attend, and it is highly unlikely that they will do other than dig still more deeply the ditch of their delusion and build more stubbornly the wall of their self-inflicted prison.

But for the truly creative person (and I refer specifically to that person capable of exercising "integral thought") LSD may be of some use. It could help him to exercise integral thought with greater ease and facility, and at will. And for a number of sensitive people willing to present themselves for a serious experiment in depth, LSD has shown itself of some help in permeating the ego, in resolving emotional conflicts, and in reducing those basic fears, the ultimate of which is the fear of death. However, the practical answer to What should be done about it? seems to be that LSD remain for the time being what it is: a "research drug," to be used with greatest care to explore the minds of those who would volunteer to aid competent researchers by offering themselves as voyagers to the "Gate of Ivory."

SEE
MANHATTAN
WHILE
IT LASTS:

A

WALKING

TOUR

Our tour begins in Wall Street,
where the Dutch built a wall and decided things had
gone far enough. So did another Dutchman, Roosevelt,
some years later.
It was built narrow, for cows.
Now it is full of bulls and bears,, and
brokers' black limousines, which are always useful
as getaway cars.
Halfway up, on the right, where you can't see it,
is Federal Hall, the spot where George Washington
was inaugurated. Well, they got that crowd out
and J. P. Morgan built across the street.
Big, substantial building with the partners all in one room,
keeping an eye on each other.
See those twin steeples* up at the end of the street?
Our clever artist, Mr. Rombola,
has put in Trinity Church there,
a good place for the rector to watch
things being rendered unto Caesar.

*Trinity has had a two-for-one split

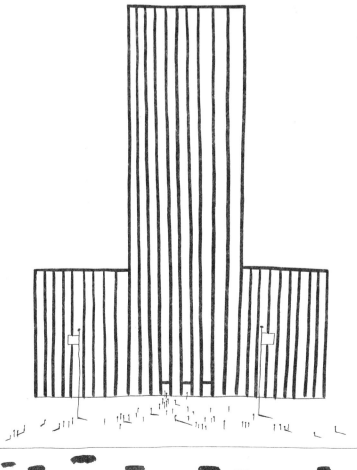

This is another period piece,
called Fifties Functional,
or Non-private Vertical. I can't tell
whether it's Seagram's, which is amber glass,
like the bottles of The Product,
or Carbide, where I suppose they make the stuff
for all those toy cannons.
See how easy it is to draw!
Just as easy to build, too. Careful!
Don't all lean against it at once!
Many buildings in New York are supposed to last
as long as fifteen years.

TEXT BY OLIVER JENSEN

Yes, it is like the Crystal Palace, somewhat,
all soaring steel and glass, but more interesting
than the row of boxes on Park Avenue
and everywhere else the modern architects build.
(They run as a pack, all in step.
Careful! No variations!)
It is a kind of temple, with tracks underneath,
the Parthenon of the Pennsylvania Railroad,
and it makes you remember that it was once
more important to be President
Thomson or Cassatt of the Pennsylvania
than Arthur or Garfield of the United States.
There is a nineteenth-century grandeur about it,
even if it was finished in 1910,
and in case this huge hall doesn't impress you,
just step into the next one,
which is like the warm room of
the Baths of Caracalla.
Vaulted roof, faded murals, great entrance hall.
Outside, long colonnades, like ancient Rome,
but all rather shabby now. Take a last look,
and close your eyes to the advertising.
Railroads aren't subsidized, and have to scrimp.
There's a new religion now, the automobile
(the trailer truck sitteth on its right hand),
and the old temples have to give way.
No sense cluttering up America's biggest city
with handsome buildings.